WORLD WAR TWO

AFVs

ARMOURED FIGHTING VEHICLES

& SELF-PROPELLED ARTILLERY

WORLD WAR TWO

AFVs

ARMOURED FIGHTING VEHICLES

& SELF-PROPELLED ARTILLERY

GEORGE FORTY

OSPREY
AUTOMOTIVE

Published in Great Britain in 1996 by Osprey,
an imprint of Reed Consumer Books Limited,
Michelin House, 81 Fulham Road, London SW3 6RB
and Auckland, Melbourne, Singapore and Toronto

ISBN 1 85532 582 9

Originated & produced by The Book Package Company Ltd.
Bournemouth, England.

Editor: Jasper Spencer-Smith

Design: John Clark, BA(Hons)

Set in 10pt on 11.5pt Monotype Bembo.

Page make-up & Reprographics by

Appletone Graphics

Bournemouth, England

Printed in Hong Kong.

ACKNOWLEDGMENTS

As always I am grateful to those who have helped me in the preparation of this book, in particular Jasper Spencer-Smith of The Book Package Co Ltd, also sincere thanks once again to David Fletcher and Roland Groom of the Tank Museum, Bovington, Dorset, England, for providing the majority of the photographs and allowing me complete access to the Museum's incomparable library. My gratitude also to Bob Fleming for supplying photographs from his collection at such short notice.

Lieutenant Colonel George Forty, OBE, FMA.

Bryantspuddle, December 1995

Title pages: A Humber armoured car, passes through the ruins of a French town, on route to Falais, France, 1944. (TM)

A total of 7720, Stug III AusFG were built in World War Two. (TM)

CONTENTS

CHAPTER ONE

Great Britain

The popularity of the armoured car with the troops in the field waxed and waned according to the various phases of different operations.... At the war peak some 24,400 carriers and armoured cars were produced per annum.

Quoted from British War Production 1939-45

British armoured cars had, with the rest of the Tank Corps, played a major part in the defeat of Germany in 1918, indeed the 17th (Armoured Car) Battalion had the privilege of leading the triumphal march to the Rhine, crossing the German frontier on 1st December 1918 and entering Cologne a few days later, the Tank Corps colours flying proudly on the leading armoured car. Postwar, despite all the cuts in the army, it was quickly realised that armoured cars were an extremely cost effective way of 'policing' the British Empire and the twelve armoured car companies of the Royal Tank Corps (RTC) served all over the world, in such distant places as India and Shanghai as well as in the Middle East, Britain and Ireland. They were assisted by the armoured car companies of the Royal Air Force (RAF), so there was a constant demand for armoured cars and many new types were built. Some of these were adapted from commercial vehicles, however, a fair number were initially designed as armoured cars and, as well as equipping RTC and RAF units, they were also offered for sale to other nations worldwide.

In the period from the late 1920s up to April 1939, when the Royal Armoured Corps (RAC) came into existence, several of the mechanising cavalry regiments were equipped with armoured cars from the outset and continued to use them throughout the war, gaining an enviable reputation for their professional expertise and bravery.

Some of the best of these cavalry regiments were undoubtedly the 'eyes' of the 7th Armoured Division (the Desert Rats), namely the incomparable 'Cherry Pickers' (11th Hussars), the Royals (The 1st Royal Dragoons), the King's Dragoon Guards and the 4th South African Armoured Car Regiment. Operating in the vastness of the Western Desert, with a continual requirement for distant reconnaissance – anything up to fifty miles ahead or to the flanks of the main body of the division – was a difficult and dangerous job at which they all excelled.

After the débâcle in France, the Reconnaissance Corps was formed in 1941 to replace the divisional cavalry regiments which had traditionally performed this reconnaissance rôle, but were now part of the Royal Armoured Corps. Regiments of the Corps fought in every theatre of war, providing reconnaissance battalions for infantry divisions, making use of reconnaissance cars, universal carriers and trucks to collect, collate and send information back, usually by radio. Their three reconnaissance squadrons were supported by both mortar and anti-tank troops, so they could give a good account of themselves when the need arose.

The popularity of armoured cars varied according to which phase of the war was in progress, for example they were considered indispensable in the Western Desert but after D-Day were little used in the close fighting in Normandy. Later on, as the front became more

mobile they returned to popularity. In Italy however, their use was always limited by the terrain. The estimated numbers of these wheeled armoured vehicles built by Britain during the war is 9,000 armoured cars, 11,000 scout cars and 8,750 light reconnaissance cars.

Scout Cars

In 1938, the Mechanisation Board invited Alvis, BSA and Daimler to submit prototypes to meet the specifications which they had laid down for a new class of turretless vehicle to be used for scouting purposes. Alvis produced the Dingo (the name went on to be used as the generic name for all scout cars but NOT this Alvis model!) which weighed 2 tons and mounted a Bren light machine gun (LMG); BSA's scout car was some 1,120lbs lighter and had a marginally inferior performance but was cheaper to produce and had a lower centre of gravity. It was chosen and went on to do very well, covering 10,000 miles during further trials without any problems. The hull was then redesigned and had a roof added – in accordance with a War Office ruling that all scout cars must be fully armoured including the roof.

The final design was then taken over by the Daimler Company, who produced the Daimler Scout Car Mk I in 1939, after an order for 172 had been placed by the War Office. Weighing

2.8 tons, fitted with a 55hp six-cylinder Daimler petrol engine, it had a top speed of 55-60mph and a range of 200 miles. The rear-mounted engine drove through a fluid flywheel to a five-speed preselector gearbox. Final drive was by four individual shafts, one to each wheel. It was 10ft 5ins long, 5ft 7½ins wide and 4ft 11ins high. It was followed by the Mk 1a (which had a folding instead of a sliding roof) and a Mk 1b (which had the cooling fan draught for the engine reversed); the Mk II which had no four-wheel steering because it had been found to be too difficult for unskilled drivers to manage. The final version was the Mk III, which now weighed 3.15 tons, had a fully waterproofed engine and the roof removed.

In total 6,626 of all marks of Dingo were produced during the war. It was an excellent, robust and reliable little two-man vehicle, and as the proud possessor of twelve of them when I commanded Reconnaissance Troop 2 RTR, I can fully vouch for their fine performance, even though I managed to get all twelve bogged down whilst route finding on my first regimental night march!

So great was the need for scout cars, that other companies, such as the Rootes Group, who built the Humber motor car, were also requested to produce them. Slightly heavier than the Dingo at 3.39 tons and larger – 12ft 7ins long, 6ft 2½ins wide and 6ft 11½ins high – the Humber scout car was similar in layout to

Above: **Prototype Alvis Dingo scout car. This was one of the two versions produced by Alvis to meet the Mechanisation Board's specifications. It weighed around 2 tons.** *(TM)*

Right: **A rear three quarter view of the second version of the Alvis Dingo. It did not have sloping top armour, but did have the same rear-mounted engine.** *(TM)*

Left: **The BSA, which was the other contender for the scout car project. It weighed 1120lbs more than the Alvis model and had marginally inferior performance, however, it was cheaper and had a lower centre of gravity. It was chosen for production, with a re-designed hull and roof.** *(TM)*

the Daimler, its engine still mounted in the rear, but it could comfortably carry three men. Top speed was 60mph and range 200 miles. Sometimes it was re-armed with a Vickers-Berthier machine gun (known also as the Vickers K). A Mk II version was even heavier, with improved transmission. A total of 4,300 Humber scout cars were built during the war.

Light Reconnaissance Cars

Humber also produced a range of other armoured reconnaissance vehicles, such as the Humber Mk I, Ironside I, light reconnaissance car. This was built on the chassis of the front-engined Humber Super Snipe, but with War Department pattern wheels, run-flat tyres and other minor changes. Three of these cars were specially modified for use by the Royal Family and cabinet ministers, and were known as 'Special Ironside Saloons'. The Humber Mk I weighed 2.8tons, had armour 12mm thick and a top speed of 45mph.

The Humber Mk II Light Reconnaissance Car, was similar to the Ironside I, but had roof armour and a small half-circular conical shield for the LMG, all of which increased its weight to 3tons. Armament was a Boys anti-tank rifle (next to the driver) and a Bren light machine

Above: **Humber MkI scout car. So great was the demand for scout cars that other firms were asked to produce them, including the Rootes Group who built the heavier (3.19 tons), slightly larger Humber.** *(TM)*

Left: **Leading a British column into Arnhem in April 1945, are three Humber scout cars from the 79th Armoured Division whose 'Bullshead' flash is painted on the front plate of the leading vehicle.** *(TM)*

Far left: **A Humber scout car leads a convoy over a Class 40 (maximum weight allowed 40 tons) bridge.** *(TM)*

gun behind the shield on top. The 0.55in calibre Boys could penetrate 21mm of armour at 300metres, five steel-cored rounds being carried in its vertical magazine. The Bren gun was the standard British infantry LMG which had a rate of fire of 500 rounds per minute (rpm) and was fed by a twenty-nine rounds top-mounted box magazine. The three-man vehicle was 14ft 4ins long, 6ft 2ins wide and 6ft 10ins high. It was followed in 1941 by the Mk III, which had a small turret instead of the shield and four-wheel drive. In total over 3,600 of all marks were built and saw service with reconnaissance regiments and also the RAF Regiment.

Another range of light reconnaissance cars was known as the Standard Car 4x2 (and by the RAF as the Car Armoured Light Standard Type-C Beaverette I). This was a 2 ton lightly armoured car, produced at the instigation of Lord Beaverbrook (hence the name) then Minister of Aircraft Production, for the defence of airfields and aircraft factories. With a length of 13ft 6ins, it was 5ft 3ins wide and 5ft high, and a top speed of 40mph. The Mk II had all-around armour – the Mk I had 3inch thick oak planks at the rear, such was the desperate shortage of metal after Dunkirk. The Beaverette Mk III was also known as the 'Beaverbug', it

Below: **A Ground Liason Officer dismounts from his immaculate postwar Daimler Dingo, 'somewhere in the desert' – possibly during Operation Musketeer – note the 'F' and French roundel also on the front of the scout car.** *(TM)*

weighed 2.6 tons, had thicker armour plate, a small turret with a hinged lid, sometimes open at the front and sometimes mounted with a plastic dome. It was 10ft 6ins long, 5ft 10ins wide and 7ft 1in high. In all 2,800 Beaverettes were built for home defence service with both the Army and RAF.

Yet another series of reconnaissance cars were built in large numbers by Morris Motors Ltd. The Mk I weighed 3.7 tons, had a crew of three and was powered by a 72hp petrol engine, giving it a top speed of 50mph. With armour 14mm thick, the car was 13ft 3½ins long, 6ft 8ins wide and 6ft 2ins high. It was followed by the Mk II, which had four-wheel drive and leaf-spring

suspension. Both were armed with a Boys anti-tank rifle and a Bren gun. Total production of both cars was 2,200. Very similar to the Mk II was the Morris Experimental Tank, which had two turrets, but never entered production.

Mention must also be made of the earlier Morris Light Armoured Reconnaissance Car (Model CS9/LAC), which was built just prewar based on a standard commercial 4x2 15cwt truck chassis. It was powered by a six-cylinder engine, which gave it a top speed of 45mph. Its armament was either a Vickers machine gun in a traversing turret, or a Boys anti-tank rifle and a Bren LMG, both of which were dismountable for ground use. The prototype was tested in 1936 and a further

Left: **Daimler scout car fitted with full amphibious equipment to both engine and crew compartment.** *(TM)*

Left: **Deep wading at Weymouth, Dorset during AFV amphibious trials held in late 1943 and early 1944.** *(TM)*

Far left: **This Daimler scout car MkIb from Regimental Headquarters 5 RTR, then serving in 7th Armoured Division, was being used by a cameraman from the Middle East Film & Photographic Unit in 1942, as he photographed a Stuart light tank.** *(TM)*

ninety-nine vehicles ordered. These were delivered in 1938. Thirty-eight of these cars were taken to France by the 12th Royal Lancers, which was the only armoured car regiment in the British Expeditionary Force (BEF), who used them to good effect during the Battle of France in 1940 protecting the flanks of the BEF. However, after Dunkirk they were all abandoned or destroyed. Thirty more were issued to the 11th Hussars, who used them in the Western Desert in conjunction with their Rolls-Royce armoured cars, some being used as light armoured command vehicles. Despite only being 4x2, it was found that the Morris CS9/LAC, once fitted

Right: **A late MkIII Dingo, which had no roof, a fully waterproofed engine and weighed 3.15 tons. This photograph was taken postwar as the Dingo remained in service for many years.** *(TM)*

Right: **A Dingo scout car under construction. Here a main hull assembly is mounted on a production welding jig.** *(TM)*

with desert tyres was ideal over soft sand. The car carried a crew of four – commander, gunner, driver and radio operator who sat beside the driver.

A range of locally modified armoured/reconnaissance cars also appeared in the dark days of 1940. These were mainly normal civilian saloon cars such as Rolls-Royce, Sunbeam and Buick, with sheets of metal fixed around them in strategic places. One which really looked the

Left: **Humber MkIII, light reconnaissance cars of the RAF Regiment in Middleburg, capital of the island of Walcheren in the Scheldt Estuary, Germany soon after its capture in November 1944.** *(TM)*

Left: **Humber MkI, Ironside I light reconnaissance car, built on the Humber Super Snipe car chassis. Three were specially modified for use by the Royal family.** *(TM)*

Below: **A Beaverette MkI, light reconnaissance car, which was also known as the Standard Car 4x2. It did not have armour all-round, the rear being protected by 3-inch thick oak wood planks!** *(TM)*

Bottom: **The Beaverette MkIII, also known as the 'Beaverbug', had better armour and a small turret. Armament is twin Vickers K aircraft-type machine guns.** *(TM)*

part was the General Motors Home Guard armoured car, a stubby, four-wheel drive coupé with a box-like hull. In addition, there were anti-tank lorries some of which were armoured with boiler-plate (Bedford OXA and Armadillo), whilst others such as Bison carried pillboxes constructed of reinforced concrete.

Armoured Cars

There were a number of obsolete armoured cars still in service when the war began in September 1939, both in the British Army and in those of some colonial forces. These included both Lanchesters and Rolls-Royce.

The massive 7.5 ton Lanchester 6x4, which first came into service in 1927, had been issued to both the 11th Hussars and 12th Royal Lancers when they were first mechanised. Later models were still in service with the armoured car companies of the Selangor & Perak Battalions of the

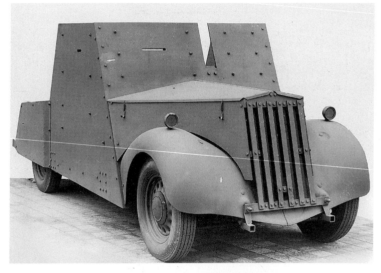

Below: **Morris MkII light reconnaissance car, a 4x2 vehicle weighing 3.7 tons with a crew of three and a top speed of 50mph. Armament was a Bren LMG and a Boys anti-tank rifle.** *(TM)*

Federated Malay States Volunteer Force (from 1938 to 1942) and also with the Singapore Volunteer Corps Armoured Car Company. They saw active service during the Malayan campaign against the Japanese in 1941–42. Turret armament was the same as that of the light tank of the period, a heavy machine gun (.50in Vickers) and one light (.303in Vickers), whilst there was a sec-

ond .303 with a telescopic sight, located beside the driver. The four-man crew of this large, cumbersome armoured car certainly had their hands full, as it had a top speed of 45mph.

The best of the obsolescent armoured cars still in service with the British Army which was used operationally, was the splendid old 3.5 ton, 1920 and 1924 pattern Rolls-Royce. Although most of them were being used for training in Britain, some of the 1924 pattern were still serving in the Middle East, where they had been taken over by the 11th Hussars, the first armoured car regiment of 7th Armoured Division. The cars had been modernised, the turret being replaced with an open-topped version with faceted armour and mounted a Boys anti-tank rifle, a Bren LMG also a smoke discharger. They had a top speed of 60mph and armour 10mm thick. These cars were used extensively for patrolling against the Italians in the Western Desert during the early days of the war.

The Guy Universal Wheeled Carrier of 1940 was an experimental vehicle, based on the Guy

Left: **Morris light reconnaissance cars on manoeuvres in Syria, October 1943. The numerals '77' denote the armoured car regiment of a Middle East Forces infantry division.** *(TM)*

Left: **A Morris CS9/LAC in France, 1940. The car, from C Squadron, 12th Royal Lancers, bears the unit code number 129 in white on a black background with a white bar, denoting Army troops. It is armed with a Bren and a Boys anti-tank rifle, both being dismountable. Note also the centrally-mounted smoke discharger.** *(TM)*

Above: **One of many improvised armoured cars constructed in Britain during the dark days of 1940. 'EAGLE' was built by the Stroud Home Guard, Gloucestershire - they adapted three civilian cars into two well-armoured cars and an ambulance.** *(TM)*

Right: **The London County Council Home Guard Battalion took over this good-looking armoured car, built in the Council's workshops during August 1940. It mounted a Vickers machine gun and carried a crew of three.** *(TM)*

Above: **The 'Tickler Tank', built using a Sunbeam car chassis by the Tickler Factory of Maidenhead, England and manned by the Home Guard. July 1940.** *(T M)*

Left: **It was amazing what could be done with some pieces of armour plate! Another Home guard masterpiece – the noise inside must have been deafening!** *(TM)*

Right: **The 7.5 ton Lanchester 6x4, first entered service in 1927. Later models were still in use at the start of World War Two and were used in action in the Malayan campaign against the Japanese in 1941 and 1942.** *(TM)*

Below: **Although obsolete and used only for training in Britain, some 1924 pattern Rolls-Royce armoured cars were deployed in action in the Western Desert during the early part of World War Two.** *(TM)*

wheeled light tank, which had an open-topped hull on a 4x4 chassis. The project was abandoned after engine cooling problems. However, a similar concept was later used by India to produce a large number of armoured wheeled carriers.

In 1938, five prototype Guy Quad armoured cars were built in mild steel by Guy Motors Ltd. This was an experimental model, based upon the Guy Quad-Ant artillery tractor chassis and trials proved most successful. They led on to the Guy Armoured Car Mk I (also called the Guy wheeled light tank). A total of 101 were built, using a welding process – the first welded armoured cars in British Army service. The first fifty mounted one .50in and one .303in Vickers MG, but the last fifty-one had BESAs (one

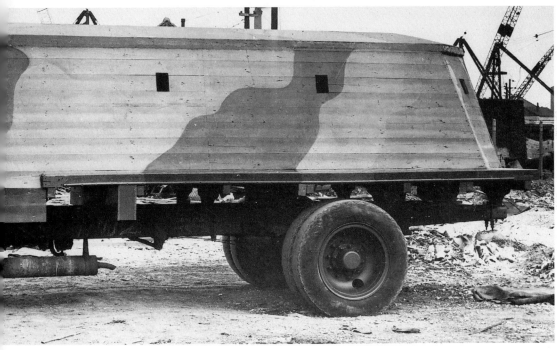

15mm and one 7.92mm) and were designated Mk IA. Weighing 5.75 tons, the 13ft 6ins long, 6ft 8ins wide, 7ft 6ins tall car, had a top speed of 35mph, a range of 210 miles and armour up to 15mm thick. A troop from the 12th Lancers, equipped with four Guys were assigned as mobile guard for the Royal family from 1940 to 1942. Two were also used by the Cabinet –

Churchill often touring London in one during some of the heaviest air raids, to encourage Civil Defence volunteers and comfort survivors.

The Rootes Group made a large number of armoured cars during World War Two, many of these were Humbers which saw service all over the world from 1941. The Mk I was very like the Guy and based on the chassis of the Karrier KT4

Top: **A Guy MkIA armoured car, mounting one 15mm and one 7.92mm BESA machine guns.** *(TM)*

Above:
The AA version of the Humber MkI, mounting four 7.92mm BESA machine guns. *(TM)*

artillery tractor which was also supplied, pre-war, to India. The first production contract for 500 was awarded in 1940. The 15ft long, 7ft 2ins wide and 7ft 10ins Mk I, weighed 6.85 tons, had a crew of three, a top speed of 45 mph and a range of 250 miles. Its armament was one 15mm BESA and a 7.92mm BESA. The Mk II, produced in 1941, had a redesigned hull, with the driver's visor built into the front plate and the radiator armour altered at the rear, all of which increased the weight by 560lbs. Armament was unaltered and the performance was very similar, as was that of the next model the Mk III,

Left: **The Humber MkI armoured car was designed using the pre-war Karrier KT4 artillery tractor chassis.** *(TM)*

Above: **The Humber MkIII still weighed about 7.2 tons, but had a larger turret, so could carry another crew member (four instead of three)** *(TM)*

Right: **Warrior is a Humber Mk IV, last of the line, mounting an American 37mm gun (the first British-built AFV to do so), which reduced the crew to three, but gave it much better firepower.** *(TM)*

which had a larger, more roomy turret which could take three men, so the crew was increased to four.

The last Humber was the Mk IV, which mounted an American supplied 37mm gun – the first British vehicle to do so – as well as the co-axially mounted BESA, however, this meant the turret could now only take two men. A modification of the basic armoured car was the Humber AA Mk I, produced in 1942, which had the original turret removed and replaced with a specially constructed one equipped with four BESA 7.92 MGs and an AA ring sight.

Based on the Dingo, the 6.8 ton Daimler Mk I was produced in 1940 and was to all intents and purposes a larger version of the scout car with a turret and a three-man crew. Main armament was a 2 pounder gun, with a co-ax BESA 7.92mm. Its 95hp six-cylinder petrol engine, gave it a top speed of 50mph and a range of 200 miles. It was 13ft long, 8ft wide and 7ft 4ins wide. The Mk II incorporated a number of modifications, such as an improved turret, driver's escape hatch, modified gun mounting and a better radiator. Nearly 2,700 were built during the war and saw service in most theatres. Armour

Above: **A Daimler armoured car, from the 1st Belgian Armoured Car Squadron, part of the First Canadian Army, photographed at Sallenelles, France in August 1944.** *(TM)*

Left: **According to the original caption, this Daimler armoured car was undergoing trials, (soon after coming off the secret list) advancing and reversing at over 40 mph, through a smokescreen and firing its 2 pounder gun.** *(TM)*

Right: **A Daimler armoured car fitted with amphibious equipment during deep wading trials held in 1944. Note the gun apron, radiator duct and flap-valve over the exhaust (submerged whilst wading).** *(TM)*

Left: **A newly-built Daimler MkI armoured car, on trials at the Daimler Car Company, negotiating difficult terrain.** *(TM)*

Left: **This Daimler armoured car is almost submerged during amphibious trials. The driver would have worn the same underwater escape apparatus as the crews of DD tanks.** *(TM)*

was 16mm thick. A regimental command version was also produced, which had its turret removed, and was known as a SOD (Sawn-Off Daimler). Finally, there was a close support version, mounting a 3inch howitzer instead of the 2 pounder. By the time the armoured cars were being used in North West Europe some of their 2 pounder guns were fitted with the Littlejohn adaptor, a device which enabled a super high velocity anti-tank projectile to be fired.

The armoured car soon took over the rôle of the light tank, but as most were only armed with machine guns and had relatively thin armour, they could not safely fight against enemy armour.

Right: **A Daimler armoured car in Malaya during the emergency there (1948-60), crossing a rickety wooden bridge. The car is from the 1st Kings Dragoon Guards.** *(TM)*

Below: **An AEC MkI heavy armoured car, which mounted a 2 pounder gun and co-ax BESA, in a two-man turret very similar to that of the early Valentine tank.** *(TM)*

The AEC Mk I, produced in 1941, was an attempt to rectify this imbalance, by mounting a Valentine tank turret, complete with 2 pounder and co-ax BESA, on a 4x4 chassis. The vehicle weighed in excess of 11 tons and was 17ft long, 9ft wide and 8ft 4¼ins high. It was a private venture produced by the Associated Equipment Company Limited (AEC), made in their factory at Southall near London. A mock-up, specially built for a vehicle demonstration on Horse Guards Parade, London made a favourable impression on Churchill.

It was followed by the even heavier (12.7tons) AEC Mk II, this time armed with a 6 pounder and co-ax BESA. The extra weight meant it needed a larger engine – a 158hp six cylinder AEC diesel, which also allowed an increase in top speed to 41mph. The front hull was redesigned with armour 30mm thick. The AEC Mk III had the 6 pounder replaced with a 75mm gun giving it a main armament comparable with many medium tanks. AEC built a total of 629 and these were deployed in the heavy troops of armoured car squadrons, to provide reconnaissance troops with heavy anti-tank support. As with the Humber, there was also an AA version, but this one utilised the Crusader

AA turret, mounting twin 20mm Oerlikon cannons. It did not enter production due to Allied air superiority after D-Day.

The Coventry heavy armoured car was an 11.5ton armoured car, built in 1944, by the combined efforts of Humber, Daimler and Commer Cars Ltd, to produce a standard armoured car to replace both the Humbers and Daimlers. It had a crew of four, armour 14mm thick, mounted a 2 pounder gun and a co-ax BESA machine gun. The Mk I was 15ft 6½ ins long, 8ft 9ins wide and 7ft 9ins high and powered by an American-built 175hp six-cylinder Hercules RXLO engine. The Mk II had a 75mm gun, reducing the crew to three. There was an even better Mk III but this was built only as a prototype. However, the end of the war came before the substantial orders placed for the Coventry could be fulfilled and the armoured car never saw action.

Although both the Staghound and Boarhound armoured cars are fully covered in the American chapter, mention of them must be made here because they were primarily built for the British Army. One interesting modification of the Staghound was the fitting of the British Crusader tank turret, which mounted

a 75mm gun, presumably to provide extra hitting power for reconnaissance units.

Armoured Command Vehicles & Gun Carriers

It was rapidly discovered that mobile armoured warfare required properly constructed and protected armoured command vehicles (ACV) from which to control operations. Command tanks were all very well for squadron and regimental commanders, but formation commanders and their staffs needed larger, roomier vehicles in which could be carried all the radio sets, maps and mapboards, plans, files and all the other equipment the staff needed to make the headquarters function. A number of modified vehicles were initially pressed into service, but eventually in 1941 a proper ACV, the 4x4 AEC Mk I was built on an AEC Matador truck chassis, powered by a 95hp diesel engine. Two of the most famous of these vehicles were used by Rommel having been captured by the *Afrika Korps* in the Desert. Known as Max and Moritz, after characters in a German childrens' story, these two *Mammuts* (Mammoths) as the Germans called them were used extensively by the Desert Fox (Rommel) who on one occasion, when his HQ was attacked by aircraft and the driver of his *Mammut* badly wounded, took over the wheel himself and drove all night.

Later in the war a new ACV was built, the Armoured Command Vehicle 6x6 AEC Mk I, which was larger than the 4x4 ACV and powered by a more powerful 150hp diesel engine. Both classes of ACVs, 4x4 and 6x6, were produced in two types: HP (High Power)

Above: **The Coventry MkII armoured car mounted a powerful 6 pounder gun instead of the original 2 pounder, which meant the crew had to be reduced to three men.** *(TM)*

Left: **The Coventry MkI armoured car was designed to replace the Daimler but the war ended before enough could be produced. The 11.5 ton, four man crew vehicle saw no active service during World War Two.** *(TM)*

Right: **A headquarters unit training in Britain, the leading armoured command vehicle (ACV) is an AEC 4x4 LP (Low Power) version. There was also an HP (High Power) version, carrying more powerful radio sets. Rommel captured and used three of these vehicles in North Africa.** *(TM)*

and LP (Low Power), depending on the range of radio sets fitted.

Also there were a number of gun carriers (such as the Foden gun carrier, AEC Deacon gun carrier, Morris AA gun carrier) and various armed jeeps - used by such fast moving units as Popski's Private Army and the Long Range Desert Group (LRDG). The former carried weapons ranging from 4-inch naval guns to 40mm Bofors, while the latter bristled with .50in and .30in Brownings, Vickers and other machine guns, giving them impressive firepower, but no armour was fitted so as not to slow them down!

Carriers

One of the most widely used and recognisable light armoured vehicles of World War Two must be the British Universal Carrier, known popularly as the Bren Carrier. However, there were in fact many varieties of this ubiquitous little vehicle, stemming from the machine gun, scout and Bren carriers of the immediate pre-war days, and stretching even further back to the light Dragon gun tractor of the early 1930s, whose ancestry goes back to the gun and supply carriers of World War One. Dragon was a corruption of 'Drag gun' which indicates the primary use of these vehicles; so they are not within the scope of this book. The carrier was really a spin-off from the development work done on the Dragon light gun tractor, by Vickers in the early 1930s, which produced a vehicle that could not only tow guns but could also carry a machine gun and its crew about the battlefield,

Left: **A T16 carrier, from the Canadian Army is being loaded into a Buffalo amphibian, behind the River Rhine dykes, March 1945.** *(TM)*

Left: **An AEC 6x6 armoured command vehicle (ACV), which was larger and more powerful (150hp diesel engine) than the 4x4. As before there were HP and LP versions.** *(TM)*

Right: **A Universal Carrier Mk II, as used by the scout platoon of a motor battalion. Note the Boys anti-tank rifle, the WS 19 wireless set (to its right), .303in Lee-Enfield rifles in their racks and other stowage.** *(TM)*

Below: **A Canadian driver repainting the vehicle signs on his carrier. It is equipped with a wading screen, which enabled it to travel through water 5ft deep instead of the normal depth of 2ft 3 ins.** *(TM)*

with a degree (albeit small) of armoured protection. The Carrier Machine Gun No 1 Mk I, which entered service in 1936, mounted a Vickers .303in machine gun and carried a crew of three in a 3.15 ton, 12ft long body, with 10mm armour but no overhead protection. The Carrier Machine Gun No 2 Mk I, which came in the following year had a Bren gun in place of the Vickers, and in some cases, also a Boys anti-tank rifle. In 1938, a range of carriers came into service:

Type	Crew	Weight	Armament
Bren No 2 Mk I & II	3	3.75tons	.303in Bren LMG or a .55in Boys anti-tank rifle
Carrier Scout Mk I	3–4	3.3tons	Boys anti-tank rifle and Bren

CARRIER ARMOURED OP – as for Scout Carrier, but with a shutter instead of the machine gun aperture, which could be adjusted to allow binoculars to be used. It was also fitted with a No 11 radio set and a cable drum (on rear). Armament was one Bren light machine gun.

GENERAL SERVICE CARRIER – this had a special grooved-rail on the top of the front gunner's compartment onto which was fixed a mobile mounting for a Boys anti-tank rifle, thus enabling the gunner to traverse through 90 degrees from front to side. A Bren was also carried.

SMITH GUN – this carried the Smith 3-inch smooth bore gun/projector which could fire both HE and anti-tank projectiles to ranges of over 275 metres. It was used by the British Home Guard between 1940 and 1942.

It soon became evident that building such a wide range of carriers was both uneconomic and unnecessary, as one basic carrier could be adapted to suit all requirements. So in 1940, the Carrier Universal No 1 Mk I (followed by the Mk II and III) came into service and remained as the standard carrier throughout the rest of the war. The basic model was a light, fully-tracked reconnaissance and combat vehicle, which had a crew of two or three, weighed 4 to 4.5 tons and had bullet-proof armour plate 7-10mm thick which was riveted at all joints. It was armed with a Boys anti-tank rifle and a Bren gun. The 12ft long, 6ft 9ins wide, 4ft 9ins high carrier was powered by a 65hp Ford V8 petrol engine which gave it a top speed of 30mph. Power was transmitted to the tracks through a standard clutch, four-speed transmission and a conventional rear-axle with sprockets instead of wheels. Steering was initiated by making lateral movements of the front bogie assembly, then by applying a brake to either sprocket so as to slow down or stop the track for tighter turns. All this was achieved merely by the driver turning the steering wheel. Its load carrying capacity was around 1,212lbs. A wide range of manufacturers built them in Britain including: Thornycroft, Morris, Sentinel, Aveling and Ford. However, demand always exceeded supply so more had to be built by Commonwealth countries.

As explained, the basic Universal Carrier was adapted to a number of uses, specific variants being designed for the following roles:

OP CARRIERS – Five versions were produced of the Carrier Armoured OP namely:

No 1 Mk II (the No 1 Mk I had been based on the Scout Carrier), No 1 Mk II, No 2 Mk III, No 2A Mk III and No 3 Mk III★. All basically had the same function, but were based on different marks of Universal Carrier. They were all FFW (fitted for wireless) - the sets were usually the No 11 and No 18, they also carried cable drums for line communications to gun positions.

Above: **A Universal Carrier fitted with a thin armoured roof. Some of the carriers in Britain were so fitted during the invasion scare of 1940. The carrier is from the Royal Gloucestershire Hussars.** *(TM)*

Left: **A line of carriers and other vehicles on training exercises in Britain. The leading vehicle is a Carrier Machine Gun LP No. 1, which mounted a Vickers medium MG in the front gun housing.** *(TM)*

addition to the driver. The mortar was merely transported over the battlefield, dismounted, assembled and went into action. Eight marks of Mortar Carriers were produced, all with slight modifications depending upon which Mark of Universal Carrier was being used.

FLAMETHROWER CARRIER – Trials in 1940 with various flamethrowing devices led to the prototype Ronson flame projector being fitted. However, this was not accepted by the War Office and was transferred to Canada. Instead, after further British development, the Wasp flamethrower was produced and fitted into a Universal Carrier. It was known as the Wasp MkI (FT, Transportable, No 2 Mk I). Its flame-gun had a range of 80-100yds and 1,000 had been produced by November 1943. A Mk II version was tested in August 1943 and proved to be a more effective flamegun. It also was safer, weighed less and was therefore adopted, seeing action in North West Europe.

MACHINE GUN CARRIERS – During 1943 it was decided to reintroduce the Vickers medium machine gun in Motorised Machine Gun (MMG) battalions, and the Universal Carrier was the vehicle selected. The gun was located on a pedestal mount, behind the driver's compartment, fitted on the strengthened engine cover. This permitted all-round traverse so the gun could be fired in any direction. In addition,

Above: **Carriers were adapted for many special uses, such as the Wasp flamethrower.** *(TM)*

MORTAR CARRIER 3-inch – In 1942, the Universal Carrier was adapted to carry the standard infantry 3-inch mortar with crew and ammunition. The mortar, baseplate and bipod were carried on the rear of the vehicle, mortar bombs in racks inside of the vehicle on both sides. The four-man mortar crew was inside, in

the normal gun tripod was carried, so that the gun could be dismounted and fired from the ground. A crew of four was also carried.

The list of uses to which the Universal Carrier was employed is endless, ranging, for example, from carpet laying devices (it carried a 150ft long roll of hessian carpet for crossing barbed wire), to

Left: **Preying Mantis was an extraordinary looking device, which had two machine guns in a head that could be raised and lowered, so as to take advantage of natural cover. The two-man crew lay side-by-side. It was never used in action.** *(TM)*

Far left: **The 3-inch Mortar Carrier No 1 Mk I - note the mortar, bipod and baseplate all strapped on the rear, whilst inside there is room for ammunition stowage and crew.** *(TM)*

swamp crossing devices with rocket assisted egress (two 5-inch rockets on the side of the carrier to literally thrust it out of bogs), to carriers with armoured roofs to protect them against enemy air attacks. Here are a few of the more useful ones:

CONGER – Evolved in 1944, this was a stripped-out, engineless Universal Carrier, into which was coiled 200yds of 2-inch hosepipe. It was towed to the edge of an enemy minefield by a Churchill AVRE, which then did a quarter right turn to allow the hose a clear run. The hosepipe was fired across by rocket, so that it lay over the minefield. Explosive liquid (Nobels 808 or 828) was then pumped into the hose from a 200 gallon tank in the empty engine well of the carrier and the hose exploded, producing a mine-free path by sympathetic detonation. There was also a smaller version, with a 1-inch hosepipe, which had the advantage of retaining its engine allowing it to be fully mobile.

AMBULANCE – With open rear end and a lengthened superstructure to allow a stretcher to be carried on either side of the engine box.

ANTI-AIRCRAFT – Fitted with an all-round traversing turret equipped with two Vickers K machine guns and a special sight.

PRAYING MANTIS – This perhaps was the strangest conversion of the Universal Carrier, fitted

with an hydraulically operated fighting compartment containing the driver and gunner, who lay side by side. On top of this compartment were two remotely controlled Bren light machine guns. In the driving position the compartment was lowered to the prone position and the driver steered the vehicle, looking through a small aperture in front of him, by means of a steering wheel (under his chest)

Above: **Pilots of an RAF fighter wing, use a Loyd Carrier to negotiate the mud on a forward airfield. Photographed in Holland, February 1945.** *(TM)*

Above: **A Loyd carrier fitted with six Bren guns in an AA mount.** *(TM)*

Right: **Carrier Tracked Mechanical MkI fitted with three drums of cable and cable feeder.** *(TM)*

and changed gear via a Bowden cable control. The Praying Mantis was designed to be driven to a suitable firing location (a hedgerow), where the fighting compartment would then be raised hydraulically and the guns fired. They could be fired singly or together, were inverted so as to allow the loading of the circular ammunition magazines from inside the compartment. The guns were fitted with a periscope-type sight.

One of the problems with the Universal Carrier was its small payload, which meant that it was invariably overloaded and underpowered. This gave rise to experimental work in both the United States and Canada, resulting in a larger version of the Universal, which was known as the Cargo Carrier T16 (later called the Universal Carrier T16). It had a bigger chassis, four bogie wheels instead of three and a more powerful engine.

The Ford Motor Company of Canada had been producing carriers, but it was the Ford Motor Company of Somerville, USA which took the job over in 1942 and completely re-designed the T16. A massive build of 21,000 vehicles was agreed for Britain and these were completed by May 1945, so not that many of them reached British and Commonwealth units before the war ended, whilst only a percentage actually saw action. The T16 never entirely found favour with the British although it was used for towing the 6 pounder anti-tank gun and carrying the 4.2inch mortar.

Left: **This Morris light reconnaissance car has been turned into a formidable vehicle, by mounting a 6 pounder gun, but there is no evidence that it was ever used in battle.** (TM)

Far left: **Developed in 1938, the Carrier Machine Gun No2 Mk I was tested as a 2 pounder anti-tank gun carrier, complete with ammunition and a crew of four. Total weight was nearly 4 tons.** (TM)

Built by Vivian Loyd and Co Ltd, and various other companies including Wolseley and Dennis, the Loyd carrier started to enter service in 1940 and was initially only used as a troop carrier (it could carry eight men), but was later used as a towing vehicle, especially for the 2 pounder anti-tank gun and later the 6 pounder. It was not as complicated mechanically as the Universal Carrier, which meant that the steering and handling was easier. Production was also undertaken by the Ford Motor Company of Canada. Weighing 4 tons, the Loyd was powered by a 85hp Ford V8 engine which gave it a top speed of 30mph. Dimensions were: length 13ft 7ins, width 6ft 9½ ins and height 4ft 8¼ ins (the hood added another 3ft 7ins). In addition to the range of troop carriers and gun tractors, there were a number of specialised Loyd carriers including:

AA CARRIER – centrally mounted platform with quadruple Brens and sighting equipment, produced in 1942-43.

SP GUN CARRIER – three versions, all mounting a 2 pounder anti-tank gun in various positions, the third being rear mounted, with a three-sided shield and some 200 degrees of traverse.

GUN/HOWITZER CARRIER – experimental only, with a 25 pounder in the front of the hull. (The Belgians tried a similar conversion postwar for a 90mm gun).

MOBILE WELDING PLANT – containing both generating plant and welding equipment.

Above: **Designed as a basic SP gun carrier, the AEC Deacon of 1942, mounted a 6 pounder gun in a flat-sided turret on the back of an AEC Matador 4x4 truck chassis. They saw active service at the end of the North African campaign and were then handed over to the Turkish Army.** (TM)

TRACKED MOBILE BRIDGE – tested in 1941, with a 30ft long bridge, capable of supporting 25-ton tanks.

Some carriers were left behind in France after Dunkirk, in May 1940, whilst others were captured in North Africa. These were taken into service by both the Germans and the Italians, the letter e in brackets was used after the German designation to signify English.

In the Wehrmacht they were used, for example, as ammunition/supply tractors (*munition-schlepper (e)*), machine gun carriers for the Maxim MG 08 (*munitionschlepper Bren fur MG 08 (e)*), anti-tank gun carrier mounting a 3.7cm PaK

Above: **The highly effective Valentine Archer SP gun, mounted a 17 pounder gun, and was one of the best anti-tank guns of World War Two. Here one guards a road near Nutterden, south east of Nijmegen, Holland during the Rhine offensive, in early 1945.** *(TM)*

(*3.7cm PaK auf Fahrgestetall Bren (e)* tank hunters equipped with *Panzerfaust (Panzerjaeger Bren (e))*.

The Italians merely fitted their own weapons, although there was an Italian carrier which closely resembled the Universal Carrier and was probably a direct copy. Finally, a few carriers were captured by the Japanese in 1941-42, some of which were converted into rudimentary light tanks, by adding plating and a small turret containing a machine gun.

It could well be said that, like the Royal Artillery, the tracked armoured carrier was to be found everywhere in World War Two. In total 50,000 carriers of all types were built by the British alone during the war years and many more were built in Commonwealth countries.

Self-propelled Artillery

In my book *World War Two Tanks* in this series, I mentioned such AFVs as the 17 pounder Archer, but did not describe it, nor the other self-propelled gun, Bishop, or to give it its full title: the Carrier, Valentine, 25 pounder gun Mk I, based on the Valentine chassis. In the same manner, whilst covering the A30 cruiser-based Challenger Tank Destroyer, I did not deal with the follow-on Avenger. This latter TD did not enter service until 1946, so although designed during World War Two, it deserves only a mention here as it saw no active service. The main reason was that the American M10 and British M10 Achilles,

mounting a 17 pounder instead of the American 3-inch gun, were already in reasonably plentiful supply. Bishop on the other hand, was a self-propelled artillery weapon, with the primary function of providing artillery support rather than direct anti-tank fire. It came into being as a result of early German success in North Africa when the *Afrika Korps* deployed, to great effect, various infantry support weapons mounted on a range of tank chassis.

This led to an urgent plea from the Eighth Army for the British to do the same. In June 1941, a scheme to mount a 25 pounder on an existing tank chassis was proposed, the Valentine was quickly chosen and, only two months later, a pilot model was produced for trials. It consisted of a Valentine tank without its turret, with a box-like, rigid armoured structure in its place, containing a 25 pounder field gun. Trials were successful, although the crew was very cramped and the gun could not achieve maximum elevation because of the confines of the box, thus restricting its range to 5,850metres (the maximum range of the 25 pounder Mk I was normally 10,900metres). After crew protection had been improved (armour thickness was eventually 8-60mm) it was rushed into service, an order for 100 being placed in November 1941, with a further 200 provisionally promised as a follow-up order.

Four months later, it became apparent to the British Tank Mission visiting the United States, led by Michael Dewar, that the Americans could

began to arrive in large numbers and eclipsed Bishop entirely. Nevertheless, Bishop continued to be used both in North Africa and Sicily, also in the opening phases of the Italian campaign. After being replaced by Priest, the Bishop continued to be used for training.

Specifications	Bishop	Archer
Weight (tons)	17.4	16.5
Crew	four (commander, gunner, loader and driver)	
Dimensions:		
Length	18ft 2 ins	21ft 11$\frac{1}{2}$ ins
Width	8ft 7$\frac{1}{2}$ ins	8ft 7$\frac{1}{2}$ ins
Height	9ft 3$\frac{1}{4}$ ins	7ft 4$\frac{1}{4}$ ins
Armament		
Main	25 pounder howitzer (32 rounds carried)	Mk I 17 pounder OQF (39 rounds carried)
Secondary	one Bren .303in LMG (AA)	
Armour thickness from 8mm to a maximum of 60mm		
Engine	131hp AEC diesel	165hp GMC diesel
Max speed	15mph	15mph
Range	90miles	90miles

produce a much better SP, namely the M7 Howitzer Motor Carriage (known as the Priest in British service), so further orders of Bishop were cancelled. By July 1942, some eighty of the first order had been delivered and the first batch had arrived in the Western Desert. At that time a further order for fifty was placed. Priests then

The success of the British 17 pounder which entered service in August 1942 despite the fact that it had to be mounted on a 25 pounder gun carriage, made it the best British anti-tank weapon (it could penetrate 130mm of armour at 915 metres). It was successfully fitted to the Sherman Firefly, M10 Achilles and Challenger A30.

Left: **Bishop mounted a 25 pounder gun on a Valentine chassis, inside a box-like rigid armour structure, which did not allow full elevation of the gun. It was later replaced in service by Priest and was then only used for training purposes.** *(TM)*

Top: **Armoured train at Derby LMS Station arouses great public interest. Note the 6 pounder gun and the machine guns in separate parts of the goods truck.** *(TM)*

Above: **This armour protected AA gun is on the back of a V8 Fordson ½ ton truck. The gun is a 20mm Hispano-Suiza.**

However, initially, investigations were undertaken to see if it would fit onto an existing British tank that was available in some quantity. Crusader was too small and underpowered, but the Valentine was suitable and its chassis was already being used for the Bishop. Initially the proposal was to use an existing turret, so as to achieve 360 degrees traverse, but neither Valentine nor any other tank for that matter at that time had a turret-ring diameter large enough to accept the 17 pounder. Using the Bishop box-like turret was also ruled out as it was too tall and unwieldy. Vickers had to design an entirely new superstructure and decided on a rearward facing mounting in a low, open-topped turret, with limited traverse (eleven degrees right and eleven degrees left) and elevation (from plus fifteen degrees to minus seven degrees). Vickers built a total of 665 Archers on Tyneside and they were used by anti-tank regiments in North West Europe and Italy. Archer carried on in British service post-war as the standard equipment of the Divisional Anti-Tank Regiment, Royal Armoured Corps.

Armoured Trains

Britain's armoured trains were nowhere near as large or complicated as those of the Soviet Union. However, they still performed a useful service, making a positive contribution to Britain's defence in the dark days of 1940 and for as long as the threat of invasion remained in the years that followed. Even such oddities as Hercules, an armoured train which operated on the Romney, Hythe & Dymchurch Railway (a passenger carrying miniature railway) in 1940, which was only 4ft 6ins high - the thought of it speeding down the track, guns blazing is enough to make Toytown tremble! However, on at least one occasion it was claimed that a member of the train's troop detachment shot down a German Me 109 fighter bomber with a Lewis gun, so it was clearly a force to be reckoned with. The more usual armoured train, which was crewed by members of the Home Guard, usually consisted of an armoured goods truck, mounting a 6 pounder gun (removed from old heavy tanks of World War One), with an extended gun shield and steel plates hinged onto the truck sides to give all round protection, while in the rear portion of the truck was a Vickers machine gun, twin Bren guns on an AA mounting and a number of riflemen. All the armoured trains had been taken out of service by November 1944.

Left: **Humber scout car, with a pintle-mounted Bren LMG. The formation sign - a red fox mask on a yellow disc, denotes 10th Armoured Division, whilst '50' shows it belonged to the armoured brigade headquarters.** *(TM/Roland Groom)*

Below: **This immaculate Lanchester 6x6 armoured car is on permanent display at the Tank Museum, Bovington. Lanchesters were still in use in Malaya at the beginning of World War Two.** *(TM/Roland Groom)*

Right & far right:
Front and rear views of the Morris Light Reconnaissance Car Mk II, which was armed with a Bren gun and a Boys anti-tank rifle. Over 3,600 of all Marks were built.
(TM/Roland Groom)

Right: **Humber Mk I armoured car. this model, built by the Rootes Group, at their factories in England. All Marks saw service in every area during World War Two.**
(TM/Roland Groom)

Right: **A Guy Mk I armoured car, built in 1939, was also known as the Guy Wheeled Light Tank. It was the first all-welded armoured car produced for the British Army.**
(TM/Roland Groom)

Above: **Praying Mantis , a conversion on the Universal Carrier chassis, which mounted twin Bren LMGs in the 'head'.**
(TM/Roland Groom)

Left: **The best British armoured car of World War Two, the Daimler, carried on in service long after the war ended.**
(TM/Roland Groom)

Right: **This immaculate Daimler Dingo belongs to Mr Nigel Care, who generously allowed it on long-term loan to the Tank Museum. it was undoubtedly one of the best scout cars of World War Two.**
(TM/Roland Groom)

Left: **A well restored Daimler scout car, photographed at a Tank Museum vehicle rally. it was an excellent, robust AFV.**
(TM/Roland Groom)

Below: **Badged for the 1st Battalion Dorsetshire regiment is this Universal Carrier, which is on permanent display at the Tank Museum. The Bren Carrier, as it was known, was one of the most widely used light AFVs of World War Two.**
(TM/Roland Groom)

Right: **Marmon Herrington Mk IV armoured car, badged for the Arab Legion. Some 2,000 were built of this excellent South African - manufactured armoured car.** (TM/Roland Groom)

Below: **A restored Sexton, the SP gun version of the Canadian-built Ram medium tank** (TM/Roland Groom)

Left: **Canada built over 3,000 Lynx scout cars during World War Two. It was almost identical to the British-built Dingo, but slightly larger and heavier. This is a MkII which had a strengthened chassis but no roof.** *(TM)*

Below: **A Canadian CMP 4x4 3-ton truck converted to a SP gun by fitting a French 75mm gun and extra armour. It was used by Free French Forces in North Africa, 1944.** *(TM)*

CHAPTER TWO

British Commonwealth

The experience of the British and Commonwealth forces
in the North African desert
campaign brought armoured cars into renewed favour.

Duncan Crow & Robert J Icks – Encyclopedia of Armoured Cars

As with tanks, although eventually Great Britain and the United States were well able to meet most of the needs of the Commonwealth countries for AFVs, this was definitely not the case when war began and also during the early years of the war. Armoured cars, scout cars and carriers did not require such heavy industry as was needed for the manufacture of tanks, so the major Commonwealth countries were, to a large degree, able to build their own vehicles.

CANADA

Canada did a quite remarkable job, producing a range of armoured fighting vehicles of quality, which included scout cars, armoured cars and carriers. Canada built a total of 200 armoured cars, 3,255 scout cars and 1,760 light reconnaissance cars during the war, a marvellous achievement.

Scout & Armoured Cars

The Lynx scout car, built by the Ford Motor Company of Canada, was the Canadian version of the Daimler Dingo, but was slightly larger (1ft 8¹/₂ins longer) and 2240lbs heavier. It was powered by a 95hp Ford V8 petrol engine, which gave the vehicle a top speed of 57mph and a range of 200 miles. Armour on the Mk I was

30mm and it had an armoured folding roof. Its dimensions were: 12ft 1in long, 6ft 1in wide and 5ft 10ins high. The Lynx Mk1 was followed by the Mk II which had various modifications, including: no folding roof, strengthened springs and axles, sand channels carried across the rear (adding some 7ins to the length). Canada built over 3,000 Lynx during the war. In addition to the Lynx Mk I & II, there was an SP artillery version, which had a 2 pounder anti-tank gun with a shield, located in the front of the Lynx body adding to its length (overall 11ft 8ins). Finally, there was the Scout Car Mk III & III★, which resembled the Lynx, built by Marmon-Herrington in the United States for Canada.

Light Reconnaissance Car Mk I Otter I was the Canadian produced version of the Humber Mk III light reconnaissance car, using mainly Canadian components and a 104hp General Motors petrol engine. Weighing 4.8 tons, the three-man Otter was 14ft 9ins long, 7ft wide and 8ft high. Over 1,700 were built and used mainly by Canadian troops in Italy, although some were supplied to the British Army and the RAF Regiment. A second version had the turret replaced by a low, bevelled shield, and was armed with a .50in Browning and a smoke mortar.

Two hundred Fox Mk I armoured cars were built by General Motors of Canada. This was the Canadian version of the Humber MkIII armoured car, armed with both a heavy and light Browning machine gun (.50in and .30in) instead

Above: **Canadian built (and manned) Universal Carrier, towing a 6 pounder anti-tank gun. The numerals '46' denote that it is from an anti-tank regiment of an infantry division, June 1944.** *(TM)*

of BESA machine guns. Dimensions were: 15ft long, 7ft 5½ins wide and 8ft 1in high. There was also a Fox Mk II which was based on the Humber Mk IV. As with the Lynx, there was also an SP artillery version, this one mounting a 6 pounder gun on a Fox Mk I chassis, in a box-like hull which was higher in front than at the rear.

Armoured Personnel Carrier GM, known also as the Truck Armoured 15cwt 4x4 GM was a small APC (only 15ft 7ins long, 7ft 6ins wide and 7ft 5ins high) with a box-like hull, raised over the driving position, open topped and had tarpaulin covered bows. On the same chassis there was an armoured ambulance which had a slightly higher hull (8ft 1½ins) and a convoy escort vehicle which was very similar to the APC, but the rear of the hull was lower.

In addition there were a number of other AFVs including: CAPLAD – British designed, Canadian-built general purpose vehicle which resembled a Fox Mk I, but without a turret. It took its name from the initials of its various intended roles: Command, Armoured Personnel, Light Aid Detachment. Development work also took place in Britain, and between 1943 and 1944 pilot models were built in both countries. However, it was really too small for use as an APC, while interest in the Command element shifted to building proper ACVs. The CAPLAD project was cancelled.

Another vehicle was based on a Canadian Ford type-AA lorry and mounted either quadruple 20mm Polsten cannons, or a partially shielded 40mm Bofors.

Carriers

The Windsor was produced in large numbers by the Ford Motor Company of Windsor, Ontario. Although the Windsor incorporated many of the Lloyd Carrier components, its design was based on the Universal Carrier. Unfortunately, some mechanical problems were discovered after the design had been approved and the agreed production of 500 a month had begun in 1943. Rectifying these faults slowed production considerably, consequently only small numbers entered service before the war ended. However, it was used in North West Europe to tow the 6 pounder anti-tank gun. As has already been mentioned in Chapter One, various models of the Universal Carrier were built in Canada (Canadian vehicles had the prefix CT rather than the normal T), as were various Medium Machine Gun Carriers (MMGC).

As also mentioned in Chapter One, the Ronson flamethrower had not been accepted for service with the British Army, but was accepted by the Canadians. Some of these Ronson devices were sent to the Pacific theatre for use in US Marine Corps M3A1 light tanks (Ronson was known as Satan by the Americans). Development continued in Canada and the

Above: **A General Motors of Canada MkI Fox armoured car, without its armament fitted (.50 and .30in Browning MGs).** *(TM)*

Wasp Mk IIC – also known as the FT Transportable No 2 Mk IIC – was developed for the Canadian Army (hence the C for Canada). The main difference to the Wasp Mk II was that only one flame fuel container (75gallons) was carried and mounted on the outside of the carrier at the rear. This meant there was room, for a third crew man inside the vehicle, who could fire a Bren gun or a 2-inch mortar. The flamegun was still the same and was mounted as for the Mk II. This allowed the carrier to be used for two rôles and not just flamethrowing. Operational use in North West Europe proved that this solution was the best and all production in Britain was changed to allow for dual capability. Sometimes plastic armour was fitted to the carrier front for increased protection.

Self-propelled Artillery

Just as the American M7 Priest was a self-propelled artillery version of the M3 medium tank, so the Sexton was a similar self-propelled artillery version of the Ram medium tank, but with the British designed 25 pounder gun in place of the American 105mm. The Sexton was developed in the latter half of 1942, motivated by the way in which the Germans managed to produce self-propelled artillery to support their *Afrika Korps* infantry. It was based on the Ram chassis, with the howitzer mounted in a central position and the driver located on the right. In order to achieve sufficient elevation, recoil had to be limited.

The pilot model was built by the Montreal Locomotive Works, shipped to Britain for trials and once approved, production began at Montreal in early 1943. By the end of that year, over 420 had been built. Additional orders continued production right up to the end of the war,

by which time 2,150 Sextons had been built. Some changes were made during production to incorporate improvements from the American Sherman, such as a one-piece cast nose, towing hook for an ammunition trailer, an auxiliary generator and mountings for Bren AA guns. As Sextons were produced they began to replace Priests in the field regiments of armoured divisions.

Specifications	
Weight(tons)	25.45ton
Crew	six (Commander, gunner, gun-layer, loader, wireless operator and driver)
Dimensions:	
Length	20ft 1in
Width	9ft
Height	8ft
Armament	25 pounder howitzer Mk II and two Bren guns
Armour	12-25mm
Engine	400hp Wright R-975 air-cooled radial
Max speed	25mph
Range	135miles
Ammunition	105rounds (HE, Smoke and stowed AP) 50 Bren magazines

Far left: **Two Canadian GM MkI Otter light reconnaissance cars, which were the Canadian version of the British Humber MkIII, here in service with the RAF Regiment.** *(TM)*

Left: **Sexton was the self-propelled gun version of the Ram medium tank. It mounted the British-designed 25 pounder.** *(TM)*

Top: **The Australian-built 4x4 scout car had a crew of two. The body had vertical sides and a sharply sloping rear deck.** *(TM)*

Above: **The Australian Rhino armoured car of 1943 mounted a 2 pounder gun in a Crusader-type turret.** *(TM)*

Right: **An Australian-built 6x6 Ford/Marmon-Herrington armoured command vehicle (ACV).** *(TM)*

Left: Australian-built Universal Carriers training in the Malayan jungle, before the Japanese invasion in 1941. (TM)

AUSTRALIA

Apart from producing a few experimental AFVs in the late 1930s, Australia had little experience of building armoured vehicles. Nevertheless, having appreciated that Britain would be unlikely to be able to fill their requirements they took on the task with enthusiasm and produced two scout cars and one armoured car between 1942 and 1943. The first Scout Car, built in 1942, was a

simply-designed turretless 4x4 car with a crew of two. The sides were vertical and the back decking sloped quite sharply. The car was 15ft long, 6ft 10ins wide and 6ft 1in high. The top had an armoured sliding roof.

The second Scout Car was known as the Rover Car and was built in 1943. Again it was turretless and low-profile in design, with an open top and covered rear wheels. It was 18ft 7ins long (the prototype had been 1ft 6ins longer), 7ft 7ins wide and 7ft high. The armoured car known as Rhino had a body that resembled a Daimler armoured car and a Crusader-like tank turret mounting a 2 pounder gun. There were three prominent diagonal bullet splash deflectors on the front glacis plate.

In addition to these three vehicles, Australia built a troop carrier which was similar to Rhino, with an open-topped hull but without a turret; a Ford/Marmon-Herrington Command Vehicle which was a 6x6 van-type command car; a utility car/cargo vehicle made by converting scout cars for use by American forces in the

Left: The turretless Rover Car was built in Australia during 1943. (TM)

Pacific. In addition, they modified the US Army White M3 scout car to make a command car, with raised body sides.

Carriers were produced in far greater quantity, with more than 5,000 being built in Australia. They decided to use the British designs and drawings, modified to suit local manufacturing conditions. Various components were made by sub-contractors with the being

vehicles assembled in State workshops. Power units were supplied from the United States. The resulting carrier was designated Carrier LP (Local Pattern).

NEW ZEALAND

New Zealand built two light armoured cars, both known as the Beaverette (NZ) Light Armoured Car. The prototype was like the British Beaverette, but built using the Ford $^3/_4$ ton chassis. The production version followed using the Ford 1-ton lorry chassis. A total of 171 were built. They also modified the American designed White M3 in the same way as the Australians, but it was called the White OP truck. In addition, they produced various unarmoured LRDG (Long Range Desert Group) vehicles, based on the Chevrolet $^3/_4$ ton truck, one type mounting Boys anti-tank rifles, Brens and light mortars; another a 6 pounder anti-tank gun, carried portee and firing over the back of the lorry!

New Zealand also followed the Australian lead as far as the production of carriers was concerned, in fact they obtained their drawings from Australia, their Ford engines and other mechan-

ical components from Canada. The carriers built were identical to those manufactured in Australia.

INDIA

Various armoured vehicles were produced by India during World War Two, including a versatile range of wheeled carriers, the first being the Armoured Carrier Wheeled India Pattern Mk I which was based on the British Guy universal wheeled carrier. The Mk II, produced in 1942, and all subsequent models were based on the a four-wheel drive chassis which was supplied by the Ford Motor Company of Canada. The Mk IIA had larger tyres, the Mk IIC was similar but with wider track, heavier components and a flat glacis with a box for the driver's head. Next came

Above: **India built a number of good, wheeled armoured carriers, this one is the India Pattern MkIIA, which was based on a Ford 4x4 chassis supplied from Canada. It mounted a Boys anti-tank rifle and a Bren AA (neither fitted in this photograph).** *(TM)*

Far left: **The prototype for New Zealand Beavertte-type vehicle, based on a Ford chassis.** *(TM)*

Left: **An Indian 2 pounder Borbette MkII. The body appears to be constructed entirely of wood!** *(TM)*

Above: **The South African Armoured Reconnaissance Car MkVI (Marmon-Herrington armoured car MkVI) mounted a 6 pounder instead of a 2 pounder gun. It was first ordered in mid-1942, but then cancelled.** *(TM)*

the Mk III, which was similar to the Mk IIB but with a partly covered hull and a small open-topped turret mounting an AA Bren gun.

The final model, the Carrier Wheeled 4x4 Mk IV (IP), was similar to the Mk IIB, but with an open hull. Its dimensions were: 15ft 2ins long, 7ft 7ins wide and 6ft high. All had similar armament, namely a Boys anti-tank rifle or Bren LMG mounted to the left of the driver and fired through a hinged flap in the front plate. The carrier had a crew of three or four, weighed 5.3tons and was powered by a 95hp Ford V8 engine. The armoured carriers were used in the Middle East, Italy and the Far East.

Produced in 1942, the 4x2 GM (Armoured Observation Vehicle (IP)) built by General Motors, had a box-like armoured body suitable for command, signals and ambulance models.

Right: **The later version of the Marmon-Herrington MkII had a welded hull with the side doors fitted further back on the body. This one was photographed in Eritrea, 1940.** *(TM)*

SOUTH AFRICA

The Union of South Africa built a series of extremely good armoured cars during World War Two, many of which saw active service in the Western Desert. Although manufactured in South Africa their engines, transmissions and suspensions were imported from the United States, while the machine guns and Boys anti-tank rifles, which formed the main armament of the early models, came from Britain, as did the later-installed 2 pounder anti-tank guns. It was the American company Marmon-Herrington, who had entered the armoured car building market in the early 1930s, which initiated the project. As well as bidding for the contract to build the T11 armoured car, they also produced armoured cars for export to Persia and developed a kit of parts for transforming commercial trucks into four-wheel drive vehicles on which could be fitted a variety of armoured bodies. A small number were purchased by the US National Guard and in 1939, the Union of South Africa chose one of their conversion kits as the basis for their new armoured car. This was a Ford 4x2 chassis, powered by a V8 engine and armoured (6-12mm thick) by the South African Iron & Steel Corporation. Known as the Marmon-Herrington Mk I armoured car (also called the South African Reconnaissance Car Mk I), it entered South African service in 1940. It had a crew of four and was armed with two .303in Vickers water-cooled machine guns, one ball mounted in a conical-shaped turret, the other in the left side rear of the hull. It had three very distinctive vee-shaped bullet splash rails on top of the bonnet. Over 100 of these cars were built but only saw service in the Union Defence Forces, none being issued to British units.

This was followed by the Marmon-Herrington Mk II, which had a longer, stronger wheelbase, a lengthened bonnet and four-wheel drive. Early vehicles had riveted hulls, but later models were all-welded. They saw service initially against the Italians in East Africa. The War Office then requested South Africa to provide them for British units in the Western Desert, where they saw service from 1941 up to the end of the Tunisian campaign. Normal armament of the Mk II was a Boys anti-tank rifle and a Bren gun in the turret, plus two AA machine guns (one Bren and one Vickers).

Although it was a very reliable vehicle it was under-gunned, so service units in the desert carried out a number of 'unofficial modifications', in order to mount a variety of captured enemy or 'acquired' Allied weapons which had a better anti-tank capability. This was done by removing the

Above: **A Marmon-Herrington MkIII armoured car, in Indian service. Built from mid-1941, the round turret of the MkII has been replaced by the octagonal-shaped type.** *(TM)*

Left centre: **A reconnaissance company of the West African Frontier Force, photographed near Accra, Gold Coast in 1943, lining up with their Marmon-Herringtons. Those in front are MK IIIs, with octagonal turrets.** *(TM)*

turret and relying on gun shields for protection, giving the added advantages of a lower silhouette and faster speed, but making the vehicle more vulnerable from the air.

Various enemy weapons were fitted, the most common being the Italian 20mm and 47mm Breda and the German 37mm and 28/20mm which had a tapered bore (like the Littlejohn adaptor). The French 25mm was also used. In addition, there were a number of other adaptations including an artillery OP (no turret), an ambulance (unarmed), a command car (no turret, hull raised to accommodate extra radios), fitters vehicle, RAF contact car (AA Lewis gun in a turret, bracing masts fore and aft to support radio antennae).

As the demand for armoured cars increased, the Mk II was replaced by the Mk III (in 1941) on the production lines, which had several improvements as a result of combat experience. It used a shorter wheelbase (8ft 9ins) and weighed 5.25 tons. Basic armament (Boys and Bren) was still the same in the octagonal turret, although similar weaponry was often fitted as for the Mk II, including the British 2 pounder and the 20mm Oerlikon. Later vehicles had only a single rear door, no radiator grilles or headlight covers. There was also a Mk IIIA, which had the turret removed and twin .303in Vickers AA fitted on a ring mount which was protected by a steel skirt. Another version fitted just one AA MG – either a Vickers or a .50in MG.

In 1943, the Marmon-Herrington Mk IV entered service. This was a completely re-designed armoured car, using Ford and Marmon-Herrington components on a 4x4 chassis. The suspension, engine and transmission were bolted direct onto the armoured hull. The

Below: **Marmon-Herrington Mk IV armoured car fitted the British 2 pounder QFSA gun and a co-ax .30in Browning in the turret.** *(TM)*

85hp Ford V8 petrol engine was located at the rear. Some vehicles were fitted with runflat tyres. The Mk IV was 15ft long, 6ft wide and 7ft high and had a top speed of 50mph and a range of 200miles. Its main armament was the British 2 pounder QFSA gun, mounted in a two-man turret, later models had a co-ax .30in Browning. In addition there were .303in or .50in Vickers MG for AA or later, .30in or .50in Brownings. Due to production delays the Mk IV did not appear until March 1943. The Mk IVF (sometimes called the Mk IV★) was very similar but had the rear-mounted engine facing forward, with the gearbox and radiator mounted at the rear. It was only issued to South African units. There was also a Mk IVF which used a CMP Ford F60L chassis. A total of over 2,000 Mk IVs were built.

A Mk V version appears not to have been produced, whilst the Marmon-Herrington Mk VI, was yet another new design. It was an eight-

wheeled armoured car which resembled the German 8 rad, with four axles grouped in two conventional bogie pairs with semi-elliptic springs mounted on trunnions. Steering was by the front and rear axles only and power was supplied by two Ford Mercury engines, mounted side-by-side with their clutches and gearboxes in the rear of the vehicle. Angled armour plates (10-30mm thick) gave good protection, whilst in the open topped turret there was either a 2 pounder or 6 pounder gun, plus a co-axial .30in Browning MG. Widely-spaced twin .30in Brownings also provided AA protection. The three-man turret had a rotating platform and electric powered traverse, but there were no observation ports for either the commander or loader. The driver had two periscopes to use when driving closed down.

It was followed by a Marmon-Herrington Mk VII, which was similar to the Mk IIIA, whilst a Mk VIII was also considered. However, as the North African campaign had ended before the Mk VI, VII or VIII entered service and as it was rightly decided that the Italian battlefield did not suit armoured cars, none of these models were put into production.

In total the South Africans built 5,746 Marmon-Herringtons, 1,180 of which were supplied to British and Indian armoured car regiments. The remainder being delivered to the Union Defence Forces and used operationally in East Africa and the Middle East. The prowess of the tough fighting men from South Africa, is ably demonstrated by the 4th South African Armoured Car Regiment, which served in North Africa with 7th Armoured Division. For example, they had been the first armoured cars to force a German tank – a new PzKpfw III, mounting a 7.5cm gun, – to surrender. Not bad for a Marmon-Herrington, armed only with a Boys anti-tank rifle and two machine guns!

Left: **This Marmon-Herrington has had the complete turret removed and an Italian 20mm Breda cannon fitted. It is being used as AA defence for the beseiged town of Tobruk, Libva.** *(TM)*

CHAPTER THREE

Germany

The development of German armoured cars had continued on a small scale since the First World War as they were the only armoured vehicles allowed to Germany under the terms imposed by the Western Allies.

Quote from Armour by Richard Orgkiewicz

Once the *Panzerwaffe* had been created in 1935, armoured cars began to be produced in quantity. Cheaper and easier to produce than tanks and with the vital task of leading the Blitzkrieg, discovering the locations of the main enemy positions then bypassing them, the armoured cars of the *Aufklarungs Abteilung* (reconnaissance battalion) proved their worth in both Poland and France. This was reinforced by their continued success in the Western Desert and led directly to a revival of interest in armoured cars, especially large heavy types, in Britain. German armoured cars were of two main types: the light four-wheeled, 3 to 4 ton *leichter Panzerspähwagen*, with a crew of two or three, an open-topped turret mounting just a machine gun or at best a 20mm cannon; and the six or eight wheeled, heavy 6 to 8ton *schwerer Panzerspähwagen*, with a crew of four, some with a fully enclosed turret mounting different weapons from a 20mm cannon to a 7.5cm gun.

Scout & Armoured Cars

The first of the new reconnaissance vehicles (*leichter Panzerspähwagen*) built for the burgeoning *Wehrmacht* was a small, 2.1 ton 4x2 scout car, built by Daimler Benz using chassis supplied by Adlerwerke of Frankfurt, known as the *Maschinengewehrkraftwagen* Adler Kfz 13. The two-man vehicle was armed with a single 7.92mm MG 13 on a pedestal mount complete with a small gunshield. It was in effect the standard small passenger car with some 8mm armour plate added and had a top speed of 44mph and a range of 187 miles. A total of 150 were built between 1932 and 1934 and saw active service in both Poland and France, but were withdrawn from service in 1941. The support vehicle for the Kfz 13 was the Kfz 14 *Funkkraftwagen* (radio car) which was exactly the same, except that it was fitted with a frame aerial and long range radio, replacing the machine gun. It had a crew of three and about forty were built. Dimensions of both were: 14ft long, 5ft 8½ins wide and 4ft 10ins high.

First of the *leichter Panzerspähwagen* SdKfz 221, 222 and 223 was the SdKfz 221, (SdKfz *Sonderkraftfahrzeug*, special purpose vehicle) designed in 1934 and issued to the scout squadrons of reconnaisance units of both Panzer and motorised infantry divisions the following year. This 4 ton, two-man scout car was the first of a highly successful series which continued to be used throughout the war. Between 1935 and 1940 a total of 340 were built. Armed with a single 7.92mm MG 34 (which became the standard Panzer machine gun in place of the MG 13), it had a top speed of 56mph and a range of 200 miles. Dimensions of the Horch engined car were: 16ft long, 6ft 6ins wide and 5ft 8ins high.

When it first came into service the scout car had to be supported by a heavier armoured car to

give covering fire, however from 1942 it was fitted with a larger weapon, this model being renamed as the Sdkfz 221 mit 2.8cm. It mounted a 2.8cm sPzB41 which had a tapered 'squeeze' bore barrel (2.8cm at the breech to 2cm at the muzzle to increase muzzle velocity – 1,430 metres per second (mps) as opposed to 1,050mps for a straight 2cm gun). The MG 34 had to be removed to mount the larger weapon. Armour was up to 8mm thick.

The SdKfz 222 three-man *leichter Panzerspähwagen* entered service in 1936 with just under 1,000 being built between 1936 and 1943. Weighing 4.8tons, it was armed with a 2cm KwK 30 or 38 L/55 gun and an MG 34 mounted co-axially. It had a larger turret than the 221 but was still 16ft long and 6ft 6ins wide, but now 6ft 8ins high. Early models were fitted with an anti-grenade mesh screen which split down the middle and could be folded outwards. Later models were fitted with a heavier gun mount which enabled the 2cm and MG 34 guns to be elevated almost vertically for AA protection. It served throughout the war on all fronts. Later models had thicker armour – up to 30mm on the nose and 10mm on the turret, instead of 8mm as standard.

The *kleiner Panzerfunkwagen* SdKfz 223 (Fu) was the radio car version (*Funkkraftwagen*) which mounted a large frame aerial around the hull and was fitted with long-range radio. The car weighed 4.4 tons, had a three-man crew, a top speed of 50mph and a range of 200 miles. It was the same length and width as the others in the series, but only 5ft 10ins high (not including aerial). The nine-sided turret mounted a single MG 34. The 223 remained in service throughout the war, providing the long-range communications necessary for reconnaisance units to transmit vitally important battle information

Entering service in 1940, the *kleiner Panzerfunkwagen* SdKfz 260 & 261 were both small radio cars developed from the four-wheeled scout car series and designed for use by headquarters units to communicate with command formations. The SdKfz 260 had a medium range radio and a rod aerial, whilst the SdKfz 261 had a longer range radio set requiring a frame aerial (this was later replaced by a rod type). The 260 weighed 3.82 tons and the 261 was just slightly heavier at 3.86 tons. Both normally had a crew of four (driver, commander and two radio operators) and because of the extra radio equipment did not have room for any armament except for the crew's issued weapons. Dimensions were: 16ft 1ins long, 6ft 7ins wide and 5ft 11ins high.

Daimler Benz had produced a cross-country lorry chassis designed for military use in 1928, which formed the basis of their *schwerer Panzerspähwagen* G3 of 1928. It had a faceted hull, weighed around 5 tons and was armed with a single machine gun. It was followed by the G3P which had better engine access (from a door in

Above: **American soldiers of 78th US Infantry Division pass two knocked-out *Jagdpanzer 38 (t) Hetzer*, whilst advancing through Kesternich, Germany, 31 January 1945.** *(TM)*

71

Above: **The SdKfz 231 *schwerer Panzerspähwagen* 6 rad. This is an early prototype model, produced in 1932. The 231 was used on active service in Poland and France.** *(TM)*

Right: **The *Maschinengewehr kraftwagen Adler Kfz 13* was the first of the new type of small reconnaissance vehicles, built by Adlerwerke in 1932 for the rapidly expanding German Army.** *(TM)*

the side of the hull) and it was the direct ancestor to the six-wheeled version of the *schwerer* 1933, the first of this type of heavy armoured car was used in action at the start of the war in Poland and later in France. In fact it had first been issued prewar, so was deployed in the annexation of both Austria and Czechoslovakia. The SdKfz 231 four-man, 5.5-ton car was armed with a 2cm KwK 30 cannon, plus a co-axially mounted MG 13. It had a top speed of 44mph and a range of 156 miles. Armour thickness was 8mm and dimensions were: length 18ft 8½ ins, 6ft 2½ ins wide and 7ft 6ins high. It was powered by a six-cylinder 60hp Daimler Benz petrol engine.

It was followed in 1936 by the SdKfz 232 (Fu) radio version which was fitted with a 100 watt long-range radio and the distinctive frame

Left & Below: **Two views of the SdKfz 222 *leichter Panzerspähwagen*. Without the anti-grenade cover fitted, the main armament 2cm KWK 30 or 38 L/550 which was mounted along with a co-ax MG34, is seen clearly.** *(RJ Fleming)*

Above: **SdKfz 139, Panzerjaeger 38(t) für 7.72cm PaK36(r),** *Marder III* **(Marten), mounted a Russian 7.62cm gun on an obsolete Czechoslovak tank chassis.**
(RJ Fleming)

Right: **SdKfz 138/1 15cm schweres Infanteriegeschütz 33 (Sf) auf PzKpfw 38(t),** *Grille* **(Cricket). Some ninety of these heavy SP infantry guns were produced in 1943.**
(RJ Fleming)

Above:
SdKfz 166 Sturmpanzer IV, *Brummbär* (Grizzly Bear). Nearly 300 of these infantry assault guns were produced and all mounted a 15cm StuH43 L/12 on a standard PzKpfw IV chassis.
(RJ Fleming)

Left: **SdKfz 131, 7.5cm PaK40/2 auf Fahrgestell PzKpfw II (Sf), *Marder II* was a useful SP anti-tank gun, which used the obsolete PzKpfw II chassis. Most were built from new, although seventy-five were converted from gun tanks.**
(RJ Fleming)

Above: **Only three prototypes were ever built of the 10.5cm le FH18/1 L/28 auf Waffenträger GW IVb, also known as *Heuschrecke* 10 (Grasshopper), an SP light field howitzer, the turret of which could be removed and placed on the ground.**
(RJ Fleming)

Above: **Mounting a lethal 8.8cm PaK43/1 (L/71) anti-tank gun on the same chassis as the *Hummel*, the *Nashorn/Hornisse* (Rhino/Hornet) first saw active service in Russia from 1943. It was later used in both Italy and Northeast Europe.**
(RJ Fleming)

Left: ***Jagdpanther* SdKfz 173, was undoubtedly one of the best tank destroyers of World War Two. Just over 390 were produced between January 1944 and the end of the war.**
(RJ Fleming)

Right: **SdKfz 184, Sturmgeschütz mit 8.8cm LaK43/2 was also known as *Ferdinand* (after Dr Porsche) or Elefant (*Elephant*). The ninety produced were built on the Tiger (P) chassis.**
(RJ Fleming)

Right: **Just eighteen of these massive 38cm RW61 auf *Sturmörser Tiger* were converted from Tiger I in 1944. Its mortar fired rocket-assisted ammunition.**
(RJ Fleming)

Right: **A well preserved SdKfz 142/1, Sturmgeschütz 40 Ausf G in the Panzermuseum collection at Munster-Oertze Germany. This was the last of the StuG series of tank destroyer/assault gun which began production at the end of 1942.**
(Panzermuseum)

Right: **Based on the PzKpfw IV chassis the SdKfz 167, Sturmgeschütz IV mounted a 7.5cm StuK40 L/48 anti-tank gun.**
(RJ Fleming)

Right: **Also on display in the Panzermuseum is *Hummel*, the 15cm schwere Panzerhaubitze auf Geschützwagen IV, SdKfz 165, a most effective SP heavy howitzer, built to provide Panzer units with artillery support.**
(Panzermuseum)

Above: **An SdKfz 221 mit 2.8cm gun of 1942. Early scout cars had to be accompanied by an armoured car to provide firepower. However, from 1942 some 220 were fitted with a 2.8cm sPzB41 gun, which had a tapered bore (2.8cm at the breech to 2cm at the muzzle) to increase muzzle velocity.** *(TM)*

Left: **The radio version of the SdKfz 222, was known as the SdKfz 223** *leichter Panzerspähwagen (funkwagen)* **and entered service 1936. Note the frame-type aerial.** *(GF)*

Above: **The SdKfz 232 6rad (Fu) was the radio version of the six-wheeled SdKfz 231. Note the distinctive frame-type aerial.** *(TM)*

Above right: **An eight-wheeled** *schwerer Panzerspähwagen* **SdKfz 231 8rad. The most powerful of all German armoured cars used in World War Two.**

Right: **The SdKfz 222 (Fu) provided long-range communications for armoured reconnaisance patrols.** *(TM)*

aerial which had a central bearing so that the hand-traversed turret could rotate freely below the antenna. Over 120 SdKfz 231 & 232 were built between 1932 and 1937, in addition a further twenty-eight SdKfz 263 (Fu), were built at the same time. This was identical to the other two except that the turret was fixed and it mounted just a single MG 13, the remaining space being occupied by additional radio equip-

ment and an extra radio operator, so the total crew was now five. It was designed for use as a radio communications vehicle and not for fighting, hence its light armament. It weighed approximately 560lbs less than the other two types and was issued to motorised signals units. After operational service in the Blitzkrieg offensives against Poland and France, the 6rad series were withdrawn from operational ser-

Above: **An SdKfz 231 8rad, captured by the British. Main armament was one 2cm KwK30 and a co-ax MG34.** *(TM)*

Left: **Based on the SdKfz 231 chassis the fully-armoured observation vehicle (*Ballistik-Messfahrzeug*) was designed to allow close monitoring of fire on artillery ranges.** *(TM)*

vice and used for training and internal security duties, because their cross-country performance was disappointing.

The ancestry of the powerful s*chwerer Panzers-pähwagen* SdKfz 231 and 232 (Fu) 8rad, eight-wheel drive armoured cars dates back to the *Mannshaftstransportwagen I* of 1928-30, when Daimler Benz, Magirus and Bussing-NAG were all asked to produce prototype eight-wheeled vehi-

cles, to be crewed by five men, be natural amphib-ians and have a good cross-country performance.

Each company built two prototypes, in fact one of Bussing-NAG's was a ten-wheel drive, larger than the others with cork-filled boxes over the wheels to assist flotation. In 1930 it was decided that the vehicle was going to be too expensive to produce, however, although the project was dropped much of the work that had

Top: **The support version of the** *schwerer Panzerspähwagen 8rad* **was the SdKfz 233 which entered service in 1942.** *(TM)*

Above: **Almost identical to the 231, the SdKfz 232 8rad (Fu) carried the usual large frame-type aerial.**

been done was used in designing the SdKfz 231 8rad four years later. Production began in 1937, of this 8.3tons (7.55 tons unladen) four-man armoured car, which was armed with a KwK30 cannon (later the KwK38) and a MG 34 mounted co-axially. The car measured 19ft 2½ins long, 7ft 3ins wide and 7ft 8ins high and was powered by a V8 155hp Bussing-NAG petrol engine. Armour was 5-15mm thick. It had a top speed of 53mph and a range of 170 miles. Over 600 were built between 1936 and 1943 of this model and the almost identical SdKfz 232 (Fu) the radio version, which had the usual frame aerial and medium-range radio equipment. Later versions of the 232 were fitted with a rod aerial on the turret and

Left: **This SdKfz 232 8rad (Fu) is fitted with a single rod-type aerial on the turret and a star-shaped aerial on the rear deck. This replaced the cumbersome frame-type aerial.** *(TM)*

Left: **British infantry, in the Western Desert, take cover beside a knocked-out SdKfz 232 heavy armoured car which has been stripped of armament.** *(TM)*

Above: **SdKfz 234/4 8rad,** mounted a 7.5cm PaK40 gun to provide close anti-tank support to other armoured cars. This one is displayed in the Panzer Museum, Munster, Germany.

Right: **Known as the Puma, the efficient looking SdKfz 234/2 mounted a 5cm KwK 39/1 anti-tank gun in the turret. Over 100 were built.** (TM)

a star-shaped aerial on the rear deck in place of the large frame-type.

Also built on the 231 chassis and probably unique was the *Ballistik-Messfahrzeug* (ballistic testing observation vehicle), a strange-looking fully-armoured observation vehicle designed for use on ranges to monitor artillery fire.

As a support vehicle to the 231 and 232 the *schwerer Panzerspähwagen* SdKfz 233 8rad was a more heavily armed version, which mounted the short barrelled 7.5cm KwK 37 L/24 in place of the usual turret. This weapon had a muzzle velocity of 2450 mps, fired a range of ammunition and greatly increased the fire support capability of reconnaisance units, despite having only limited traverse. Six of these vehicles were included in each reconnaisance squadron. Fully laden the three-man 233 weighed 8.58 tons, had a top speed of 53mph, a range of 187 miles and measured 19ft 6ins long, 7ft 3½ins wide and 7ft 6ins high. A total of 109 were built between 1942 and 1943.

Panzerfunkwagen SdKfz 263 (Fu) 8rad was the eight-wheel drive version of the 263 6rad with a fixed turret, no armament except for a single machine gun, allowing room for more radio equipment and an extra radio operator. Between 1938 and 1943 a total of 240 were built and were issued to signals units of Panzer and motorised divisions also to some specialised formations. Like the 6rad version it was designed as a radio car, hence its purely defensive armament.

Work began in the early 1940s to produce a successor to the 231 series and the first models

Left: **The SdKfz 234/3 8rad mounted the short-barrelled 7.5cm KwK 51 L/24 gun – under ninety were built.** *(TM)*

entered production in 1943. Although the *schwerer Panzerspähwagen* SdKfz 234/1 and 234/2 8rad were similar to the previous series it had one major difference being of monocoque construction, – integral body and chassis unit. Thicker armour up to 30mm on the front of the hull was used, while the 220hp Tatra 102 diesel engine gave the 11.5 ton vehicle a top speed of 50mph and a range of 375 miles. Range was later increased to 625 miles by fitting a larger fuel tank. All two hundred 234/1s, produced between 1944 and 1945 mounted a 2cm KwK 38 gun and a co-ax 7.92mm MG 42 (now the new Panzer machine gun). The vehicle's dimensions were 20ft long, 8ft wide and 7ft high.

The best of the heavy eight-wheeled armoured cars built by the Germans was the SdKfz 234/2 Puma, designed to allow the Wehrmacht the ability to stand up to Soviet light and medium armour. It mounted a 5cm KwK 39/1 gun and co-ax MG 42 in a turret originally designed for the Leopard light tank. Only 101 Pumas were built (1943-44), but it saw service in four Panzer divisions both in North West Europe and on the Eastern Front, being organised into *Panzerspähwagen* companies of twenty-five Pumas each. It measured 22ft 7ins long, 8ft wide and 7ft 7ins high.

Taking over the rôle of the 233, in providing the heavy support for reconnaisance units, the *schwerer Panzerspähwagen* SdKfz 234/3 and 234/4 8rad was an open-topped car mounting a 7.5cm KwK 51 L/24 short-barrelled gun with limited traverse. It was followed by the 234/4 which mounted the longer, even more powerful 7.5cm PaK 40 L/46 gun, complete with gunshield. Almost 180 of the two types were built, approximately ninety of each model.

Wheeled APC's & Miscellaneous Vehicles
schwerer Gelandegangiger gepanzerter personenkraftwagen SdKfz 247 Ausf A & Ausf B – Approximately

Right:
Sturmgeschütz 40 Ausf G (also called the Stug III Ausf G) assault gun\tank destroyer negotiates a Soviet anti-tank ditch. The main armament was the 7.5cm StuK 40 L/48 gun. Note also the armoured shield on the machine gun by the loader's hatch and the peri-binoculars on the commander's cupola.
(TM)

sixty of these wheeled APCs were built using a heavy passenger car chassis. Both could carry six men. The Ausf A was a six-wheeled, four-wheel drive vehicle, weighing 5.2 tons and the Ausf B four-wheel drive weighed 4.46 tons. They were used mainly as armoured staff cars by the commanders of reconnaisance battalions. No radio or armament was fitted. A top speed of 44mph (Ausf A) and 50mph (Ausf B) was achieved and both had a range of 250 miles

Strassenpanzerwagen – The *Waffen SS* made up a number of improvised armoured personnel carriers/armoured cars for use in internal security roles, while the police used the Austrian-built ADGZ.

schwerer Gelandegangiger lastkraftwagen fur FlaK (Sf) – A self-propelled anti-aircraft gun which mounted the 3.7cm FlaK 36 or 5cm FlaK 41, (the latter probably only in prototype form) on a Mercedes-Benz L4500A, four-wheel drive heavy truck chassis, with

armour fitted around the driver's cab. Other types of trucks were used to mount the smaller 2cm AA gun.

schwerer Minenraumfahrzeug – Built by Krupp in 1944, this massive 130 ton mine clearing vehicle had wheels over nine feet in diameter, on which the heavily armoured body was carried The wheels were set out on different track widths from front to rear, so that they covered a wider path, exploding mines by pressure.

Tracked Self-propelled Guns

As with their halftracks, the Germans made wide use of all their Panzer chassis to mount a variety of self-propelled guns (*Selbstfahrlafette* (sf)), including assault guns (*Sturmgeschütz*), infantry assault guns (*Infanteriegeschütz*), anti-tank guns (*Panzerjaeger*), anti-aircraft guns (*Flakpanzer*), SP

Top: **The massive 130-ton mine-clearing vehicle (*schwerer Minenraumfahrzeug*) was built as a prototype only by Krupp in 1944.** *(TM)*

Above: **The Commander of a Stug III Ausf G company takes the salute as his troops move to the battle front.** *(TM)*

Right: **One in every eight or nine Stug III Ausf G was fitted with the heavier 10.5cm howitzer and designated the *Sturmhaubitze 42 (Stu 42)*. A total of 1,200 were produced.** *(TM)*

Right: **This battle photograph of a Stug III Ausf G (StuK 40) gives a good view of the PzKpfw III chassis and suspension on which the AFV was based.** *(TM)*

Above: **The 10.5cm leFH18/1 L/28 auf Waffenträger GW IVb, was better known as the *Heuschrecke* (Grasshopper) 10. Only three prototypes of this tracked light field howitzer were built in 1943.** *(TM)*

Left: **The 15cm heavy infantry gun was mounted on the hull of the PzKpfw I Ausf B to produce the 15cm siG33 (Sf). These were photographed near the Desna River in Russia** *(GF)*

field howitzers or guns (*Feldhaubitze* and *Feldkanone*), assault howitzers (*Sturmhaubitze*), assault mortars (*Sturmmörser*) and tank destroyers (*Jagdpanzer*). They also did the same with a wide range of captured enemy equipment. This followed a deliberate policy which had begun in the mid-1930s and was not just some haphazard way of finding new uses for obsolescent tank chassis. Perhaps the most important of these were the *Sturmgeschütz*, with their dual capability as assault guns and the anti-tank rôle. The *Panzerjaeger* (tank hunter) was used offensively and rose to prominence especially in 1942, as a result of meeting masses of Soviet tanks when the Germans began their invasion of Russia.

PzKpfw I Chassis

Some 200 PzKpw I Ausf Bs were modified in 1940-41 by removing the turret and mounting a 4.7cm PaK(t) L/43.4 anti-tank gun, the (t) – *tchechoslowakisch* – denotes that the gun was of Czechoslovak origin. This was the first of many such conversions and prolonged the service life of the obsolescent PzKpfw I chassis. It saw service in France and the Low Countries in May 1940 and went on being used until late 1943. The gun had limited traverse (twenty-five degrees) and elevation (minus eight degrees to plus twelve degrees), with a three-sided open-topped gunshield, to give a small amount of protection to the three-man crew. Weighing 6.4 tons, it had the same dimensions as the PzKpfw I Ausf B, except that it was 10ins higher. It was designated as the *4.7cm PaK(t) (sf) auf PzKpfw I Ausf B*.

During early 1940, approximately thirty *15cm siG33 (Sf) auf PzKpfw I Ausf B* heavy infantry guns were produced by removing the turret and fitting the 15cm siG33 L/11 heavy infantry gun in a large box-shaped gunshield some 10mm thick, which added 2ft 8½ins to the normal height of the PzKpfw I Ausf B. The vehicle's weight nearly doubled to 8.5 tons and carried a four-man crew. The gun was on its normal artillery carriage and the shield was open at the top and rear. Maximum elevation was seventy-five degrees and traverse twenty-five degrees. Only twenty-five rounds of amunition were carried. As with the 4.7cm they were used in the Blitzkrieg of May, 1940 and continued in service on the Eastern Front. The 15cm gun had a maximum range of 4,700 metres.

PzKpfw II Chassis

A small number, only twelve, *15cm siG33 auf Fahrgestell PzKpfw II (Sf)* heavy infantry guns were produced in late 1941, using a specially widened and lengthened PzKpfw II chassis, measuring 18ft long, 8ft 8ins wide and 6ft 4ins high, so the vehicle was lower than the PzKpfw II except when the gun was elevated. The lengthened chassis carried an extra roadwheel on each side but was otherwise unchanged, even though the total weight was increased by over 1 ton to 11.2 tons. The superstructure had 30mm thick armour in front and 15mm on the sides. The gun had fifty degrees of elevation and twenty degrees traverse. Thirty rounds of ammunition were carried. All were deployed by the *Deutsches Afrika Korps* in North Africa.

In 1942, the *Wehrmacht* decided to develop a self-propelled version of their standard 10.5cm leFH18M field howitzer to provide fire support for their Panzer divisions. They chose the obsolescent PzKpfw II chassis, building the *SdKfz 124 Leichte Feldhaubitze 18/2 auf Fahrgestell PzKpfw II (Sf) Wespe* (Wasp) as it was designated, on a slightly lengthened chassis with only three top rollers instead of four and spring loaded bumper stops for the road wheels. The

superstructure armour of the 11.7 ton *Wespe* was 20mm thick in the front, 15mm at the sides and 8mm at the rear. The driver was seated well forward, separated from the three-man gun crew. Although 1,000 were initially ordered only 676 were eventually built, between 1943 and 1944. They first entered service about the time of the great Kursk tank battle and remained operational for the rest of the war. A further 159 munitions carriers (*Munitions-Selbtsfahrlafette auf Fahrgestell PzKpfw II*) were built and carried ninety rounds of ammunition, in support of *Wespe* which carried only thirty-two rounds. The vehicle measured over 16ft long, 7ft 7½ins wide and 7ft 8ins high, had a top speed of 25mph and a range of 137 miles. The gun had forty-five degrees of elevation, thirty-four degrees of traverse and a maximum range of 10675 metres.

The name *Marder* (Marten) was given to three self-propelled anti-tank guns during World War Two, *Marder I* and *Marder III* both mounting foreign manufactured weapons while the *Marder* II fitted the German 7.5cm PaK40/2 mounted on the PzKpfw II chassis. This was produced as a deliberate attempt to upgun the obsolescent PzKpfw II and of the 651 produced, only seventy-five were converted the rest being built from new between June 1942 and June 1943. The conversions followed when production was switched to building *Wespe*. The 10.8 ton, four-man SP had an open-topped box-like superstructure with 30mm thick armour in front and 10mm on the rest. It had a top speed of 25mph and a range of nearly 120 miles. The *Marder II* entered service in July 1942 and continued to be used in action for the rest of the war. Its gun could penetrate

92mm of armour plate at 900 metres. Thirty-seven rounds (both AP and HE) of ammunition were carried Its German designation was *SdKfz 131 7.5cm PaK40/2 auf Fahrgestell PzKpfw II (Sf) Marder II.*

The *SdKfz 132 Panzer Selbstfahrlafette I fur 7.62cm PaK 36(r) auf Fahrgestell Ptzkpfw II Ausf D und E* mounted a captured Soviet 7.62mm PaK 36 anti-tank gun, which had been fitted with a muzzle brake and re-chambered so that it could fire German PaK 40 ammunition (thirty rounds carried). A large number of these guns had been captured early in Operation Barbarossa and when firing the PaK 40 ammunition it could penetrate 80mm of armour plate at 900 metres. The SdKfz 132 weighed 11.5tons had an open-topped 15mm thick armoured super-structure which extended over the whole length of the vehicle. The gun, still fitted with

Above: **The 7.5cm PaK40/3 auf PzKpfw 38 (t) Ausf H (SdKfz 138) was a self-propelled anti-tank gun on the Czech-built chassis. Over 400 were in service (175 being converted from tanks in 1943, the rest built from new). They served in Russia, Tunisia and Italy.** *(TM)*

the normal shield, fired over the superstructure and could traverse fifty degrees and elevated from minus five degrees to plus sixteen degrees. Approximately 200 were converted between April 1942 and June 1943.

PzKpfw 38(t) Chassis

Built in 1943 the *SdKfz 140 leichte Flakpanzer 38(t) auf Selbstfahrlafette 38(t) Ausf M* was the very first German (ex-Czechoslovak) full-tracked vehicle to be used for an AA weapon. The gun chosen was the 2cm FlaK 38 which fired both HE and AP tracer, to an effective ceiling of 3200 metres, fed from a twenty round magazine. Rate of fire was 180-220 rounds per minute (rpm) and a total of 1040 rounds were carried. The gun had all-round traverse and could elevate to ninety degrees. One hundred and forty of these 9.8ton, 16ft 2½ins long, 7ft 1ins wide and 7ft 6ins high AA tanks were produced between late 1943 and early 1944. It had a top speed of 25mph and a range of 115 miles.

The *SdKfz 139 Panzerjaeger 38(t) fur 7.62cm PaK36(r) Marder III* was again the simple use of an obsolescent tank chassis to mount a larger

anti-tank gun, the Soviet 7.62cm PaK36 on the Czechoslovak-built TNHPS chassis (thirty ammunition rounds carried). In 1942 a total of 344 were built and later a further nineteen were converted from gun tanks. Weighing 10.6 tons, the *Marder III* measured 19ft 6ins long, 7ft 2½ins wide and 8ft 1in high, so it had a high silhouette and very little protection for the four-man crew. Over 2240lbs heavier than the gun tank, the vehicle had to be re-engined with the more powerful 150hp EPA-2 engine. It entered service in July 1942 and was deployed on the Eastern Front and also in North Africa.

In early summer 1942, it was decided to build a new SP gun, again based on the 38(t) chassis, but this time mounting the German 7.5cm PaK40/3 L/46 anti-tank gun instead of the Russian 7.62cm. The prototype of the *SdKfz 138 7.5cm PaK40/3 auf PzKpfw 38(t) Ausf H* was ready in June 1942 and was fitted with an improved superstructure, giving better crew protection. With a crew of four, the 10.7 ton vehicle had a top speed of 25mph and a range of 115 miles. Its main armament could be elevated from minus five degrees to plus twenty-two degrees and traversed sixty-five degrees each side in the forward arc. Firing APC (forty rounds carried,

plus thirty-eight HEAP) the gun could penetrate 76mm of armour at 2300 metres. Armour plate on the superstructure was 10-15mm thick and the SdKfz 138 measured just under 19ft long (including gun), 7ft wide and 8ft 3ins high. Approximately 240 were built between 1942-43. A further 175 were converted from gun tanks in 1943. They were deployed to the Eastern Front, also in Tunisia and Italy. Of those built eighteen were exported to Slovakia.

The *SdKfz 138 Panzerjaeger 38(t) mit 7.5cm PaK40/3 Ausf M* was the largest of the early production *Panzerjaeger* on the 38(t) chassis and was a better designed version mounting the German 7.5cm Pak40/3 L/46 gun and was also called the *Marder III*. It came about after Hitler had personally ordered all 38(t) production to be switched to building SPs (so a complete redesign was possible) to replace the models built to date. The major change was to move the engine to the middle of the chassis, thus enabling the gun to be mounted at the rear, making it more stable, more manoeuvrable (as the gun did not overhang) and lighter (10.5tons) because the frontal armour did not need to be as thick. The resulting Marder III was built between April 1943 and May 1944, but when after 975 had been built it was replaced by the *Hetzer* (Baiter). It saw service on all Axis battlefronts of the war from May 1943 onwards.

As the war on the Eastern Front progressed, it became clear that there was a need for a light tank

Below: **Another use of the 38(t) chassis was to mount a 2cm FlaK 38 L/112.5 AA gun, and was designated as the Flakpanzer 38 (t) auf Selbstfahrlafette 38 (t) Ausf M (SdKfz 40).** *(TM)*

Right: **One of the best light tank destroyers, the 15.75ton *Jagdpanzer 38 (t) Hetzer* (Baiter) which mounted a 7.5cm PaK 39 L/48 gun in a low, streamlined chassis.** *(TM)*

Below: **Grille (Cricket) was yet another SP infantry gun which used the excellent 38(t) – either Ausf H or M – chassis. Between 1943 and 1944 a total of 232 were built.** *(TM)*

destroyer (*Jagdpanzer*) to replace the existing both towed and self-propelled light anti-tank guns. Indeed, General Heinz Guderian, Inspector of Armoured Units, was calling for one to be designed as early as spring 1943. Development was centered upon a widened TNHP chassis, as the running gear of *Hetzer* was about ten percent larger, with a track width of some 1ft 2ins as it had to carry the extra 5 tons weight of the heavily armoured bodyshell – armour was 20 to 60mm thick. When built the *Jagdpanzer 38 (t) Hetzer* was 15.8 tons in weight, 21ft 3½ins long (including gun), 8ft 9ins wide and 7ft 2½ins high. The gun was a 7.5cm PaK39

L/48 which was offset to the right in the sloping front plate, the driver seated to its left and the rest of the four-man crew in the fighting compartment. Traverse was only five degree left and eleven degrees right, so the vehicle had to track to engage targets. Forty-one rounds were carried in the vehicle. An MG 34 or MG 42 was mounted on the roof and remotely controlled from inside the vehicle. *Hetzer* had a top speed of 24mph and a range of 110 miles, it first entered service in July 1944 and fought for the rest of the war. After the war it was used by both the Czecholsovak and Swiss armies. From April 1944 onwards 2,584 were produced.

Two adaptations of *Hetzer* were built, the *Flammpanzer 38(t) Hetzer*, twenty being converted by fitting a 14mm *Flammenwerfer* in place of the 7.5cm anti-tank gun and the *Bergepanzer 38(t) Hetzer* armoured recovery vehicle, sixty-four being converted to this rôle. With the gun removed and a winch fitted in the fighting compartment, it was deployed in tank hunting units equipped with *Hetzer*.

The *SdKfz 138/1 15cm schwerer Infanteriegeschütz 33(Sf) auf PzKpfw 38(t) Ausf H Grille* (Cricket) carried a 15cm siG33/1 L/12 heavy infantry gun mounted on the rear-engined 38(t) Ausf H chassis (as Sd Kfz 138). Ninety of these

11.5tonners were produced during early 1943, all had a crew of five and a top speed of 22mph. Issued to *Panzergrenadier* regiments from early 1943, it saw service in all European and other battle areas. Eighteen rounds of ammunition were carried for the 15cm gun which had seventy-three degrees of elevation and ten degrees of traverse on its mount and a maximum range of 4,700metres. It was followed by a second type of Sd Kfz 138/1 *Grille*, which used the Ausf M chassis. A further 282 were built of this slightly heavier type(12tons) the *15cm schwerer Infanteriegeschütz 33/1 auf Selbstfahrlafette 38(t) (Sf) Ausf M*, which like its predecessors saw service on all fronts for the rest of the war.

Munitionspanzer 38(t) (Selbstfahrlafette) Ausf M was the tracked ammunition carrier needed to back up *Grille* which had a small ammunition carrying capacity. The plan was to have two of these with each detachment of six *Grille* as they could each carry forty rounds of 15cm ammunition. Between January and May 1944 a total of 102 were built.

PzKpfw III Chassis

As early as 1936 it was decided that Panzer divisions needed mobile assault and anti-tank guns

Sturmgeschütz (StuG) of at least 7.5cm calibre. The PzKpfw III light/medium tank chassis was chosen as the basis, but mounting the low velocity 7.5cm gun of the PzKpfw IV. Later, higher velocity guns were mounted which made it possible to achieve both the assault gun and the self-propelled anti-tank gun rôles. From the outset the StuG was designed as a dual purpose weapon system. The StuG Ausf A (Sd Kfz 142) was the first to be produced in early 1940 and was followed by the Ausf B, Ausf C und D, and Ausf E, all being armed with the short-barrelled 7.5cm StuK37 L/24 gun. The Ausf F entered service mounting the

long-barrelled 7.5cm StuK40 L/43 or L/48, making it a lethal anti-tank weapon as well as an assault gun. This type (allotted a different *Sonderkraftfahrzeug* (SdKfz) – special purpose vehicle number – SdKfz 142/1) continued through Ausf F/8, Ausf G then onto the StuH42 (Sd Kfz 142/2), which mounted the more powerful 10.5cm gun. There were also a few flamethrowers (StuG III), assault guns (StuG 33B) and ammunition carriers. Approximately 680 of the early type of StuG III were built, over 8,500 of the dual purpose StuG III and over 1,210 of the *Sturmhaubitze* 42 (StuH42). The largest build of the series was that of the Ausf G, 7720 being built and a further 170 plus converted from gun tanks. Tank aces, such as Michael Wittmann, learned his skills commanding one of the first StuG IIIs to be allocated to the

Leibstandarte SS Adolf Hitler, knocking out many enemy tanks on the Eastern Front.

Specifications	StuG III Ausf A	StuG III Ausf F	StuH42
Weight (tons)	19.6	21.6	24
Crew	four	four	four
Dimensions			
Length:	17ft 11ins	21ft	20ft 5^1/$_2$ins
Width:	9ft 8^1/$_2$ins	9ft 8^1/$_2$ins	9ft 8^1/$_2$ins
Height:	6ft 6ins	7ft 2ins	7ft 2^3/$_4$ins
Armament	7.5cm StuK37 L/24	7.5cm StuK40 L/43 or L/48	10.5cm StuH 42 L/28
	and one MG 34 or MG 42		
Armour	up to 50mm up to 80mm with *Saukopf*★a		
Engine	Maybach HL 120TR	Maybach HL 120TRM	
Top speed	all 25mph		
Range	100miles	100miles	97miles

a. this was a large cast gun mantlet, nicknamed by crews Saukopf (pig's head) because of its shape.

PzKpfw IV Chassis

As with the PzKpfw III chassis, the ubiquitous PzKpfw IV was also used as the mount for a wide variety of guns, including anti-tank, infantry assault, self-propelled artillery and anti-aircraft. In the first of these categories there were five main *Panzerjaeger*, which are summarised in the following table:

Name	Armament	
StuG IV	7.5cm StuK 40	L/48
Jgd Pz IV	7.5cm PaK 39	L/48
Pz IV/70 (V)	7.5cm PaK 42	L/70
Pz IV/70 (A)	7.5cm PaK 42	L/70
Nashorn (Rhino)	8.8cm PaK 43/1	L/71

PaK: *Panzer abwher Kanone* (anti-tank gun)

The first of these, the StuG IV came into being as a result of heavy bombing halting StuG III production at the Alkett works. Also Hitler ordering that PzKpfw IV production should be stopped so that Krupp could instead manufacture StuG IVs. They produced their first vehicle in December 1943 and it proved to be an excellent assault gun or tank destroyer, weighing 23 tons with a top speed of just under 24mph and a range of 130 miles.

The very similar, but slightly more streamlined *Jagdpanzer IV* was produced by Vomag as a successor to the StuG III and was first issued to *Panzerjaeger* units in March 1944, seeing service in Russia and later in Normandy. Weighing over 2240lbs heavier than the StuG IV, it had approximately the same performance but its frontal armour was only 60mm instead of 80mm thick. The two PzKpfw IV/70(V) & (A) were built as improved models of *Jagdpanzer IV*, both mounting the long-barrelled version

Top: **Hummel (Bumble Bee) was a 15cm heavy howitzer on the PzKpfw IV chassis. This is the prototype vehicle built by Alkett.** *(TM)*

Right: **Wirbelwind**
(Whirlwind)
mounted the four-
barrelled 2cm
FlaKvierling in an
open-topped fully-
traversing turret.
Only two of the
four guns are
fitted. *(TM)*

Below: **Probably
the best tank
destroyer in any
World War Two
army was the**
Jagdpanther
**(SdKfz 173).
The low, sleek
silhouette,
excellent
performance and
lethal 8.8cm
PaK 43/3 L/71 gun
made it a first
class tank killer.**
(TM)

of the 7.5cm anti-tank gun. The (A) – Alkett version was 2 tons heavier at 28 tons (thicker armour on the lower hull), but they were otherwise very similar in appearance. The (V) – Vomag version *Nashorn* (Rhino), on the other hand was entirely different to the other four, being built to provide a suitable SP version of the 8.8cm PaK43 gun. It used the same basic chassis as the *Hummel* (Bumble Bee) and proved to be a highly effective tank killer, with a top speed of 26mph and a range of 135 miles.

Just under 300 of the infantry assault gun *Brummbär* (Grizzly Bear) were manufactured between 1943 and 1945 with a few more being converted from gun tanks. This version of the StuG IV mounted a 15cm Stu43 L/12 short-barrelled assault howitzer in a box-like superstructure, weighed some 28.2tons, carried a crew of five and had a top speed of 25mph. It first saw action at Kursk, Russia but was then deployed on most fronts, including Italy. The howitzer had a maximum range of about 6400 metres and a total of thirty-eight rounds of ammunition were carried.

The *Hummel* had a lengthened PzKpfw IV chassis modified to mount a 15cm sFH18/1 L/30 heavy howitzer centrally in an open-topped, box-like turret. The resulting vehicle weighed 24tons and carried a crew of six. Only eighteen rounds of ammunition could be carried, further supplies being transported in a *Munitionspanzer* built on the same PzKpfw IV chassis. About 100 self-propelled guns and 150 munitions carriers were built and issued to artillery formations, especially on the Eastern front. The gun had fifteen degrees of traverse each side of centre, a maximum elevation of forty-two degrees and a range of 12,550 metres. Further experimental work was also carried out, resulting in three light SP field howitzers, all mounting the same 10.5cm leFH18 howitzer. None entered production.

There were four *Flakpanzer IV* which saw service in World War Two, two with the name of *Möbelwagen* (Furniture Van) – one version mounting the four-barrelled 2cm FlaKvierling 38 gun, the other a 3.7cm FlaKvierling 43.

Left: **Thirty-six PzKpfw IV were converted into *FlaKpanzers*. They mounted the 3.7cm FlaK 43/1 and was known as *Ostwind* (East Wind).** *(TM)*

Below: **Badly damaged, this 65-ton *Elefant* (Elephant) heavy assault gun, stands in a shattered Italian town's main street, it's 8.8cm gun silent forever.** *(GF)*

Both had all-round traverse and could be elevated to ninety degrees. When the vehicle was moving the folding sides enclosed both the gun and gun crew, but were dropped to a horizontal position when preparing for action, thus extending the fighting platform. *Wirbelwind* (Whirlwind) mounted the four-barrelled 2cm FlaKvierling 38 in an open-topped octagonal revolving turret, whilst *Ostwind* (Eastwind) had a 3.7cm FlaK 43/1 gun in a six-sided open-topped turret. In total, under 400 *Flakpanzers* of all four types were produced or converted, main production version was the 3.7cm FlaK *Möbelwagen* of which 240 were produced between 1944 and 1945. Just before the war ended, a satisfactory light *Flakpanzer*, known as *Kugelblitz* (Ball Lightning) was designed and built, but production never started due to the cancellation of PzKpfw IV production in mid-1945. Only two prototypes were ever built, both mounting twin 3cm guns in a round turret.

Mention must also be made of perhaps the strangest adaptation of a PzKpfw IV in the ammunition carrying rôle, which was as the carrier for *Karlgerät* the massive 124 ton tracked siege mortar (see later). The *Munitionsschlepper für Karlgerät* could carry only four of the 60cm rounds, each weighing around 2 tons, stored in racks mounted around the engine compartment. The vehicle was also fitted with a crane to lift the shells. Only twelve PzKpfw IV Ausf F1 were converted in 1941.

PzKpfw V Chassis

Jagdpanther (Hunting Panther) was without doubt one of the most successful conversions of any standard tank chassis into a heavy tank destroyer, (the 8.8cm PaK 43/3 L/71 gun having a formidable offensive capability) on what was a streamlined, well-armoured chassis powered by an excellent engine. Only 392 of these superior vehicles were produced from January 1944 onwards and first saw action in June 1944. They were organised as a troop in heavy anti-tank battalions, which comprised three companies each of fourteen vehicles, with three more in battalion headquarters.

According to the official German handbook, *Jagdpanther* was designed as the *Schwerpunkt* weapon for the destruction of enemy attacks. To achieve this rôle they had to remain constantly mobile and not be committed as static anti-tank guns except in a dire emergency. After completing their mission, they were to be withdrawn for repair and maintenance, then held ready for the next emergency. The 33ft long (including gun) *Jagdpanther* was 11ft 5ins wide and only just over 9ft high – nearly 12ins shorter than Panther. The 46-ton vehicle had a crew of five, armour up to 100mm thick, a top speed of just under 30mph and a range of 125miles.

PzKpfw VI Chassis

The massive Tiger chassis was used for three very different weapon systems, the first being *Tiger-Mörser* a heavy assault mortar; the second a heavy assault gun/tank destroyer adapted from one of the failed Tiger prototypes (Tiger (P)) known as both *Elefant* and *Ferdinand*. Lastly the *Jagdtiger*, the heaviest most powerfully armed tank destroyer to see action in World War Two.

Only eighteen *Sturmmörser Tiger* were ever built, these mounted a 38cm StuM RW61

L/5.4 assault rocket mortar (*Raketenwerfer 61*), which had been developed for the German Navy by Rheinmetall-Borsig for use in anti-submarine warfare. The mortar was housed in a large box-like structure, with armour up to 150mm thick. The breech-loading weapon was slightly offset to the right and could traverse only ten degrees either side of its centre-line. Elevation was up to eighty-five degrees and, although range varied very much with charge temperature, maximum attainable range was around 5900 metres. There was a seven-man crew for the 65-ton *Sturmmörser Tiger*, a commander, a forward observer, a driver and the four-man mortar crew. Designed to fill a requirement for infantry support in street fighting, they were used mainly in the defence of Germany.

During the development of Tiger, both Henschel and Porsche produced their prototypes of the VK4501 and it was the Henschel VK4501(H) that was chosen. However, a production order was already well advanced for ninety VK4501(P) – also called Tiger(P) – at Nibelungwerke, Linz, Austria. It was decided to make good use of most of these chassis by fitting new superstructures, more armour and the long-barrelled 8.8cm PaK 43/2 L/71 anti-tank gun. This work was carried out by the Alkett works at Berlin-Spandau, Germany. In order to mount the gun properly it had to be fitted on the rear of the chassis in a large fixed turret. The

Below: **Largest and most powerfully armed fighting vehicle of World War Two to see operational service was the 70-ton *Jagdtiger* (SdKfz 186), which could easily knock-out any enemy tank with its 12.8cm PaK44 L/55 gun, whilst the 250mm thick front glacis made it relatively invulnerable to enemy fire.** *(TM)*

Left: **The *Tiger-Mörser* mounted a massive 38cm mortar and weighed 65 tons. Only eighteen were ever converted from Tiger 1's during 1944. It fired rocket-assisted, mortar ammunition originally developed by Rheinmetall-Borsig for the German Navy to be used in anti-submarine warfare.** *(TM)*

resulting *StuG mit 8.8cm PaK 43/2 (SdKfz 184)* also had its original Porsche engines replaced by two production Maybach HL 120TRM tank engines. Known initially as *Ferdinand* (presumably after its designer Dr Ferdinand Porsche) it

was later called *Elefant* (Elephant) – an apt name for a vehicle weighing 65tons, with armour 200mm thick on its hull front. It first saw action at Kursk in May 1943 and quickly gained a reputation for its lethal firepower.

Specifications

	Jagdpanther	Elefant	Jagdtiger
Weight (ton)	46	65	70
Crew	five	six	six
Dimensions			
Length:	32ft 10½ins	22ft 11ins	34ft 11½in
Width:	10ft 11ins	1ft 1in	12ft 1in
Height:	9ft 1in	9ft 10ins	9ft 5ins
Armament	8.8cm PaK 43/3 L/71	8.8cm PaK 42/2 L/71	12.8cm PaK 44 L/55
Armour	17-80mm	30-200mm	30-250mm
Top speed	28mph	12mph	22mph
Range	30miles	95miles	100miles

Most formidable of all tank destroyers used in World War Two was the 70-ton *Jagdtiger*, which used the chassis of the Tiger II rather than the Tiger I to mount a massive 12.8cm PaK 44 L/55 gun. Firing APCBC, the gun could penetrate 178mm of armour plate at 1800 metres. Armour was up to 250mm thick on the front plate of the fixed turret. The gun had a small amount of traverse – ten degrees each way and could elevate from minus seven and a half degrees to plus fifteen degrees. Entry for the six-man crew was at the rear, through a hatch with double doors. The main drawback was its powerplant, the same 700hp Maybach HL230 as used in both Panther and *Jagdpanther*. Whilst this excellent engine gave both lighter AFVs a good performance, it was underpowered for a TD some 27tons heavier, especially when travelling cross-country. Seventy-seven *Jagdtigers* were produced between July 1944 and March 1945. Due to a shortage of 12.8cm guns, some had to be fitted with the same 8.8cm gun as *Jagdpanther*. Issued to only two combat units, it saw service in the Ardennes and in the defence of Germany.

Foreign Chassis

The Germans mounted a range of anti-tank and self-propelled artillery on some of the chassis captured by them early in the war.

French chassis.

Lorraine tractor 37L	7.5cm	PaK 40/1 anti-tank gun
	10.5cm	le FH18(Sf) field howitzer
	15cm s	FH13/1(Sf) field howitzer
FCM 36 light tank	7.5cm	PaK 40/1 anti-tank gun
	10.5cm	le FH18(Sf) field howitzer
Hotchkiss light tank	7.5cm	PaK 40 (Sf) anti-tank gun
	10.5cm	le FH18(Sf) field howitzer
Renault light tank	4.7cm	PaK(t) anti-tank gun
Char B1bis heavy tank	10.5cm	leFH18/3(Sf) field howitzer

British chassis.

Bren Carrier	3.7cm	PaK anti-tank gun three 8.8cm anti-tank rockets
Light Tank Mk VI	10.5cm	le FH16(Sf) field howitzer
Matilda Mk II	5cm	KwK L/42(Sf) gun

Sf – *Selbstfahrlafette* – self-propelled gun mount
KwK – *Kampfwagen Kanone* – tank gun

Ammunition Carriers

In addition to the specialised ammunition carriers (*Munitionsschlepper*) which have already been covered (*Wespe*, *Grille* and *Karlgerät*), there were a number of other general ammunition carriers based on various tanks chassis from PzKpfw I to PzKpfw III. They included for example, the *Munitionsschlepper auf PzKpfw I Ausf A*, which was a PzKpfw I without a turret, the resulting

circular hole being covered with armour plating (segmented) so as to provide overhead cover for the driver and his load. Fifty were converted in early September 1939 and used by supply companies of Panzer units in both Poland and France.

Next came the *Munitionsschlepper Ausf PzKpfw 1a und 1b*, which was an obsolete PzKpfw I with a large steel box (complete with a canvas cover) replacing the turret. The turrets from these and all the other *Munitionsschlepper* were not wasted, some were used on permanent fortifications. Several hundred of these small, but most valuable ammunition carriers were issued to Panzer divisions from 1942. The Czech-built PzKpfw 38(t) was similarly converted and from 1942 onwards, over 400 of these extremely useful load carriers being made available as the *Munitionsschlepper auf Fahrgestell PzKpfw 38(t)*. Old PzKpfw III

were used in the same way (as well as being converted into fitters vehicles, artillery OP and command vehicles, the resulting *Munitionspanzer III* then being issued to Panzer supply units.

Finally, mention must be made of the conversion of a number of StuG III later in the war, between 1944 and 1945, which had the main armament removed and the open front plate covered with additional armour, and designated *Munitionspanzer auf Fahrgestell StuG III Ausf G*.

Mine Clearing & Explosives Carrying Vehicles

Some of the smallest tracked vehicles in the Wehrmacht fall into these two very similar categories, *Minenraumwagen* and *Ladunsträger*

Left: **Goliath SdKfz 303 leichter Ladungsträger** was a remotely controlled, expendable tracked demolition charge vehicle, of which there were two types, this is the heavier version. For long-distance transportation it could be carried on a purpose built two-wheeled trailer. *(TM)*

Left: **SdKfz 301 schwerer Ladungsträger Ausf A/B** was much larger than *Goliath*, weighing 3.6 tons. It was designed to be driven to a target where the demolition charge (on the front of the vehicle) could be dropped, the vehicle withdrawn and the charge remotely exploded. *(TM)*

both of which were given the same prefix letter (B) in OKH nomenclature. The SdKfz 300 unmanned, *Minenraumwagen* was an expendable, remotely-controlled mine-clearing vehicle built by Borgward from 1939 to 1940 and weighed 1.5tons. There were two versions, known as BI and BII, the earlier model towing a number of rollers, each weighing 30lbs, intended to detonate mines. There was also an amphibious version called *Ente* (Duck) but it never progressed beyong the experimental stage. Fifty of both BI and BII were produced but none saw combat service, all being replaced by *Goliath*.

There were two versions of the *leichter Ladunsträger Goliath*, the first being the SdKfz 302, which was 6ft long, 2ft 8ins wide and 2ft high. It weighed 816lbs and was powered by two electric motors, (one to run each track) propelling it at speeds of up to 6mph with a range of around 1600 metres. It was steered by two strands of a three-strand cable, the remaining strand was for detonating the 132lbs explosive charge it carried. Over 2600 were built between 1942 and 1943.

The second model (SdKfz303) weighed 948lbs and carried 220lbs of explosive. Powered

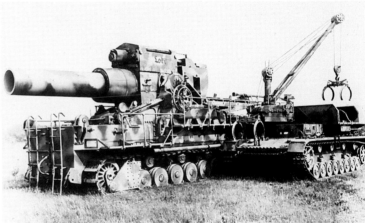

Above: **The other type of mortar barrel fitted was the 54cm Gerät 041 L/11.5. Both the 54 and 60cm barrels were interchangeable. Only seven guns in total (including one prototype) were built and at least four were used on active service.** (TM)

the target then dismount, close down the turret to protect the radio receiver which was then used to guide the vehicle to its target and also to detonate the explosive.

Heaviest of the three types was the *schwerer Ladunsträger (SdKfz 301)*, built by Borgward between 1942 and 1944. A total of 570 of the Ausf A, B & C being produced, of which the Ausf C was the heaviest (4.8tons), most numerous and had the most powerful engine. All could carry 1,100lbs of explosive, a crew of one had a top speed of 25mph and a range of 132 miles. The Ausf C was just over thirteen feet long while the earlier, lighter (3.4 tons) models were shorter. All were radio-controlled and used in much the same way as the *Springer*.

Tracked Heavy Seige Mortars

From the smallest tracked vehicle in service to the largest, *Karlgerät* the self-propelled heavy seige mortar of which one prototype and six production models were built. Weighing 124 tons, it measured 38ft long, 10ft 6ins wide and nearly 16ft high. It mounted either a 60cm Gerät 040 L/8.44 mortar or a 54cm Gerät 041 L/11.5 mortar (the latter had almost double the range – 12,500 metres as opposed to 6,675 metres). They fired either concrete-piercing or high explosive shells. The mortar was mounted on a tracked chassis with eleven roadwheels and powered by a 44.5-litre Daimler Benz engine which gave it a top speed of just over 6mph. Built in the period 1940 to 1941 and given the name *Karl* (after General Karl Becker of the Artillery who was involved with its development), they saw action on the Eastern Front, most notably at Sevastopol, Lvov and Brest-Litiovsk. Two were captured by the US Army in Bavaria. The six production *Karlgeräts* were named: *Adam und Eve*, *Thor und Odin*, and lastly *Loki und Ziu*.

by a 703cc motorcycle engine, it could travel at speeds of up to 7.5mph and had a range of over 12,000 metres. It was a great improvement on the earlier model and over 4,900 were produced.

Next in size and weight came the *mittlerer Ladungsträger (SdKfz 304) Springer* produced by NSU, some fifty were built between late 1944 and early 1945. It weighed 2.4 tons was 10ft long and had a crew of one. The 1.5-litre four-cylinder Opel Olympia petrol engine gave it a top speed of 26mph and a range of 125 miles. It could carry 728lbs of explosive. The technique was for the crew to drive the *Springer*, as near as possible to

Left: ***Karlgerät* was a large self-propelled heavy siege mortar, weighing around 125 tons. It mounted a 60cm Gerät 040 L/8.44 mortar, which could be fired at a maximum rate of six rounds per hour.** (TM)

CHAPTER FOUR

United States

In the United States, the use of armored cars by the cavalry had barely begun when their role was largely taken over by tracked vehicles. The operations in Africa revived the development of armored cars in the United States.

Armour by Richard M Ogorkiewicz

With the start World War Two a period of massive rearmament began in the United States, which included the provision of all types of AFVs for the Armored Force. As part of the overall programme a special Armored Vehicle Board (the Palmer Board), was formed, with the task of evaluating all the available models. Comparative testing took place between late 1942 and early 1943, after which the Board decided that an armored car would be defined as: 'an armored wheeled reconnaissance vehicle weighing not more than seven short tons'. This resulted in the cancellation of most of those AFVs proposed with only a few left in production. In a similar manner, a large number of different types of self-propelled guns and howitzers were designed and built in the United States, but many were just prototypes or produced in small numbers of around 100, which were then used only for extended testing, but failed their acceptance tests. Nevertheless, the Gun Motor Carriges (GMCs) and Howitzer Motor Carriages (HMCs) which were produced and built in significant numbers, made a major contribution to Allied battlefield successes. Other AFVs, such as carriers did not have quite so many problems, the T16 and the M28/M29 (Weasel) both being produced in large numbers.

Although the Americans built a number of different armored cars during World War Two – nearly 16,500 in total – many of these were for export to Britain and not for their own use. Apart from the M8 Greyhound of which nearly 3,000 were built, the US Army did not use armored cars, but preferred to reconnoitre either in halftracks or jeeps – the latter being closely followed by a tank. Close battlefield reconnaissance was invariably performed in a tank, armored protection being preferred to stealth. There were of course reconnaissance units, some of which built quite a reputation for themselves – such as a Third Army unit which earned the nickname; *Patton's Household Cavalry!* This unit was Colonel Edward M Fickett's 6th Cavalry Group. It comprised a number of reconnaissance platoons (each two officers, twenty-eight men, six armored cars and six jeeps). Their task was to send back a steady stream of up to the minute battlefield information, which their HQ would then teletype direct to Patton's forward headquarters, so that he was usually better informed than anyone else about any situation!

As well as tanks, the American armament industry also produced large numbers of a wide range of AFVs which were then generously supplied to their Allies: the British Army, the Red Army, the Chinese and many others benefited from the United States. For example, the Red Army was supplied with 3,340 M3A1 scout cars, over 1,800 mechanised guns and nearly one hundred T16 carriers. The British even had an armored car built almost exclusively for their own use, over 2,400 Staghounds were delivered and over 1,600, 3-inch GMC M10s along with 830, HMC M7s served with the British Army.

Scout Cars

The notion of having a wheeled, light vehicle with which to carry out reconnaissance was first seriously considered by the US Army in 1897, when Royal P. Davidson, then professor of tactics at Wisconsin Military Academy, designed the Davidson Duryea, which fitted a .45 Colt automatic machine gun with an armored shield mounted on a small, motorised, commercial tricycle chassis. It was followed in 1898 by a four-wheeled vehicle. In the 1920s and 1930s a series of open-topped civilian cars – Pontiacs, Chevrolet and Studebaker – which had been fitted minimal armor and a pintle-mounted machine gun, were built in small numbers. From this developed the T7 scout car of 1934, built by the White Motor Company, which was the first of a long line of highly successful scout cars leading in 1938 to the development of M3.

The M3A1 was the only scout car to be built in any significant numbers – 20,918 being produced during World War Two. Although it has already been covered in a companion volume to this book: *World War Two Military Vehicles Transport & Halftracks* by G N Georgano, I must also include it here for completeness as it was the most important American-produced scout car.

Its ancestry goes back through the long line of armored scout cars, built by the White Motor Company, such as the T7 (M1) Scout Car of the early 1930s. The final form of the White scout car could be seen in the M2A1, which was tested by Ordnance in September 1937. A second wheeled version was built in 1938, at the same time as the halftrack was being developed at the Rock Island Arsenal, Illinois. The M3 scout car had a skate-type mount for a the .50in heavy machine gun in front and fitted a .30in machine gun at the rear. It had increased in weight to 4.45tons, could carry eight men and had a top speed of 65mph. The M3A1 first shown in 1939, was now powered by a 110hp Hercules petrol engine, weighed 3.85 tons was fast and reliable and was used for a wide variety of tasks, including gun towing and also as an ambulance Final dimensions were 18ft 5½ins long (with a sprung-roller front bumper) 6ft 5½ins wide and 6ft 3ins high.

Other versions were: M3A1E1 with a Buda diesel engine in place of the Hercules JXD petrol engine; M3A1E2 with a mock-up armored roof; M3A1E3 which had a pedestal mounted 37mm gun behind the front seats; M3A1 Command Car, built in 1943 with an armored windscreen, a .50in HMG and built-up armored sides.

Chrysler also produced a simple 'add-on armor' scout car in 1941, built for convoy protection or as a small APC, the armored body being bolted on to a Dodge 1½ton 4x4 truck chassis. However, due to problems with its narrow body and high silhouette, it did not enter production.

During the development of the 4x4 Jeep, a larger ¾ton 6x6 version was built as a cargo carrier or ambulance and other uses. Smart Engineering Company of Detroit also produced the

Above: **Leading a supply convoy on the approaches to the River Po, through the rubble of war torn Ponteloscuro, Italy, April 1945, is an M3A1 scout car in service with the British Eighth Army.** *(TM)*

Right: **During training exercises in the United States, probably prior to America entering the war, a column of M3A1s cross a pontoon bridge.** *(TM)*

Below: **M3A1 scout car fitted with the standard .50in Browning heavy MG at the front and a .30in at the rear, both on pintle mountings.** *(TM)*

T24 scout car, an armored version of the 6x6, weighing 2.4tons. Its armament was a single .50in Browning heavy machine gun on a pedestal mount in the centre of an open-topped with all-round sloping armor. After testing, it was decided not to proceed, as there was considered to be no requirement.

As well as various field conversions of the Jeep, with add-on armor which have also been covered in Georgano's book, there was a series of scout cars designed and built by the Smart Engineering Company, which used the standard Willys 4x4 chassis. First in the series was the Smart scout car, built in 1941, which was

Above: **One of the 'Lend-Lease' M3A1 scout cars delivered to the Soviet Union, being used to tow a small field gun.** *(TM)*

Left: **Photographed in 1938 these early M3A1 scout cars show clearly the spring-roller front bumper. The leading car mounts a water-cooled .30in Browning machine gun.** *(TM)*

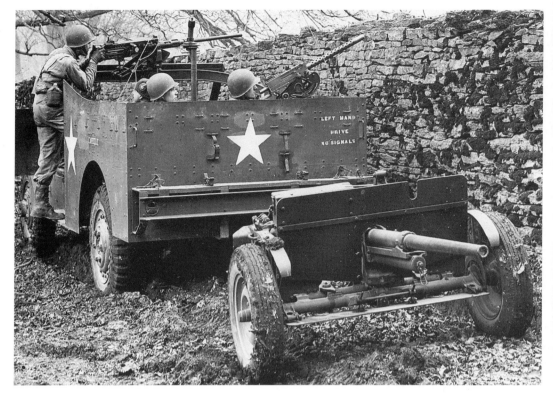

Right: **M3A1 towing a 37mm anti-tank gun, as the crew prepare to engage the enemy with their Browning machine guns.** *(TM)*

Below: **White M3A1 scout cars on parade with the Brazilian Army shortly after that country's declaration of war on 22 August 1942.** *(TM)*

followed by the T25, the T25E1, T25E2 and T25E3. All had slightly different armor configurations, the last one being 12ft long, by 5ft 5ins wide and 4ft 11ins high. It had better cooling for the radiator, hinged side and rear armor, while the bonnet armor extended forward so that in appearance it resembled the Russian BTR-40 built after the war.

There were also a number of small cars, such as the Observation Post Tender T1 & T2, small 12ft long vehicles built by Ford for use by intelligence gathering personnel. They all weighed around 3tons and were powered by a 90hp Ford engine. Another was the Fort Meade Car (also known as the Howard Johnson Car and as the Blitzwagen), which looked similar to the M3

Right: **The T24 scout car was produced by Smart Engineering in 1942. It was 14ft long and armed with a .50in Browning machine gun on a pedestal mount. It did not enter production.** *(TM)*

Far right top: **Observation Post Tender T1 was built by Ford and intended for use by intelligence gathering personnel.** *(TM)*

Far right centre: **The Observation Post Tender T2 weighed 6600lbs fully laden and was better armoured than the T1, but never entered production.** *(TM)*

Right: **The T25 scout car was produced on the Willys Jeep chassis by Smart Engineering in 1942. It was 14ft long and armed with a .50in Browning machine gun on a pedestal mount. It did not enter production.** *(TM)*

scout car, built on a Ford chassis, with a .50in machine gun on the top of the hull, rifle ports at the sides and a rear ramp for loading a wheeled 37mm anti-tank gun.

A third was the John Deere Model A armored tractor of 1941, which was a small agricultural-type tractor with an armored bonnet, flat-shaped armor covering for the driver, small front wheels and larger rear ones, measuring 11ft 5in high, by 8ft wide and 7ft 8in wide. It was designed for use as a prime mover in areas where hostile fire could be expected. Tested at the Aberdeen Proving Ground (APG) in 1941, the 4.25 ton vehicle was both cumbersome and slow, so was eventually deemed unsuitable for military use.

Four-wheeled Armored Cars

The Chevrolet Division of General Motors, Detroit, Michigan built the Staghound, a four-wheeled armored car to specifications agreed between the US Armored Force command and the British Army staff in Washington. It was designated the T17E1, because the T17 design

and development number had been allocated to the Ford Deerhound. An order for 3,500 was placed to be shared between the British and Americans, however, the US Army cancelled their smaller share. Fortunately for the British Army, production continued and over 2,400 were eventually completed and shipped to Britain. The 13.7 ton, 4x4 Staghound was powered by two six-cylinder 97hp GMC

Above: **The John Deere Model A armored tractor of 1941, was based on a small agricultural vehicle. It never entered service.** *(TM)*

Right: **New ready for delivery T17E1 Staghounds which were, according to the original photograph caption, '......a closely-guarded military secret'.** *(TM)*

Right: **Staghound equipped with Bantu – a system for mine locating, which employed electro-magnetic rollers front and rear.** *(TM)*

petrol engines, which gave it a top speed of 56mph and a range of 450 miles. Staghound carried a crew of five and was an extremely robust and useful vehicle. It was 18ft long, 8ft 10ins wide, 7ft 9ins high and was armed with a 37mm gun and a co-ax .30in Browning machine gun. There was another .30in MG in a ball mounting in the hull and a third on an AA mounting on top of the turret. Armor thickness was 9.45mm.

The standard armored car was followed by an AA version, the T17E2, which had a completely new turret designed by Frazer-Nash in Britain mounting two .50in Brownings. The Frazer-Nash D8394 hydraulically-operated open turret had all-round traverse and was fitted with

Above: **T17E2 fitted with the British-designed Frazer-Nash D8394 open-topped turret mounting twin .50in machine guns. A total of 100 were produced.** *(TM)*

Left: **Staghound fitted with a British Crusader tank turret, mounting a 75mm gun and co-ax BESA machine gun.** *(TM)*

a gun-mount which allowed the guns to elevate to seventy-five degrees and depress to ten degrees. One hundred were built. Staghound was also modified to mount a 75mm howitzer, but this was only built as a prototype and never entered production.

Six-wheeled Armored Cars

As explained, about the same time as Chevrolet were building Staghound the Ford Motor Company were, in 1942, designing and build-

ing the 6x4 Deerhound armored car, which was allocated the T17 designation. The 12.5 ton armored car had a welded hull and was 18ft long, 8ft 9ins wide and 7ft 10ins high. It was powered by two six-cylinder 110hp Hercules engines and carried a crew of five. Armament was a 37mm gun and co-ax machine gun in a M24A1 combination mount, fitted in a T-7 light tank turret, plus another ball-mounted .30in MG in the front of the hull. It was offered to Britain but they opted for the smaller Staghound. Eventually 250 Deer-hounds were built.

Right and below:
Left and right views of the T17 Deerhound armored car which was designed and built by Ford at the same time as Chevrolet were building Staghound. It was fitted with the same turret as the T7 light tank. *(TM)*

Another six-wheeler was the T19, built by Chevrolet in 1942 which, like the T17 was fitted with the light tank turret. Weighing 12.5 tons, the T19, had six equally spaced axles mounted on large vertical coil-springs. It was followed by the T19E1, which had a better mounting for the 37mm gun but weighed 1,000lbs more. Dimensions were 18ft 4ins long, 10ft wide and 8ft high. It was powered by two V8 260hp Cadillac engines.

In 1942 Studebaker built the T21 a 6x4 armored car in the 7 to 8 ton range, which was also known as the GMC (Gun Motor

Above and left: **Front and rear views of the Studebaker-built T21 6x4 armored car of 1942. It was also designated as the T43 GMC.** *(TM)*

Left: **The Chevrolet-built T19 armored car of 1942, fitted the turret of the T7 light tank (as the T17). The vehicle's 104hp engine gave it a top speed of 50mph.** *(TM)*

Right: **The M8 Greyhound, was the United States most widely deployed armored car. Armament was a 37mm gun with a skate ring-mounted .50in Browning heavy machine gun on top of the turret.** *(TM)*

Far right top: **The T69, based on the M8 chassis, had quadruple .50in Maxson AA MGs mounted in an open-topped turret.** *(TM)*

Far right centre: **The T22 armored car, built by Ford was developed as the T22E1, then as the T22E2 which was the prototype for the M8.** *(TM)*

Carriage) T43. It was not as successful on test as other models built around the same time, notably the Ford T22. The complete armored top to the driver and co-driver's compartment hinged downwards.

At 6.7tons the four-man, Ford-built T22 of 1942, was lighter and smaller (dimensions were 15ft long, 8ft 4ins wide and 6ft 8ins high) than many of the other contenders. It was armed with a 37mm M6 gun and co-ax .30in MG in an M23 combination mount, with no form of stabilizer fitted, so firing on the move would have been extremely difficult. The driver's cab had a folding armored top. Development of the T22

led on to T22E1 and eventually to T22E2, which was the prototype for the Greyhound.

The United States' most widely used armored car of World War Two was the M8 Greyhound. Built by the Ford Motor Company of St Paul, Minnesota the M8 weighed 7.6tons, and was both fast (top speed 56mph) and quiet,

making it ideal for reconnaissance operations. Its dimensions were 16ft 5ins long, 8ft 4ins wide and 7ft 5ins high. Powered by a rear-mounted six-cylinder 110hp Hercules JXD petrol engine, the four-man Greyhound was armed with a 37mm gun and co-ax .30in machine gun, mounted without a stabilizer in a manually traversed turret.

Above: **The crew of an M8 Greyhound observe enemy positions.**
(TM)

121

Above: **The M20 armored utility car, of which nearly 4,000 were built by Ford. A versatile machine with a .50in heavy machine gun on a skate-ring mount.** *(TM)*

Right: **The Trackless Tank of 1940 was built only as a prototype by the Trackless Tank Corporation. Later in 1941-42 the T13 was produced, employing many features from this design.** *(TM)*

There was no hull machine gun, but a turret-mounted AA MG was fitted. A total of 8,523 were built and a reasonable number were used by the British Army. An M8E1 followed, which had slight suspension changes and a skate-ring mount added for the .50 AA machine gun. The GMC T69, was another version of the M8 which mounted quadruple .50in Maxson machine guns in a multi-sided, open-topped, power-operated turret for AA defence.

Ford also built nearly 4,000 of the M20 armored utility cars, which were also based on the T22 and known variously as the T26 and M10 armored utility car as well as its final designation M20. In place of a gun turret it mounted a .50in Browning heavy machine gun with a

Left: **Reo built three prototypes of the T13 in 1941 all mounting the same 37mm gun and a co-ax MG.** *(TM)*

skate-ring mount, on what was the M8 chassis, so there was no overhead cover for the crew. It was used for a variety of purposes, including both as a command car and an APC. Also there was an experimental version which mounted twin .50in Brownings.

In 1942 the Chrysler Corporation also built the T23 armored car in competition to the T22. It looked very similar to the Ford T22, but had a large, high armored cowl over the driving compartment, which interfered with the depression of the main armament.

Built in 1944 as a successor to their T19E1, Chevrolet produced the good looking T28 armored car, which weighed 6.5tons and had a top speed of over 60mph. It was also sometimes called the Wolfhound. It was later designated as the M38 armored car, mounting a 37mm gun and .30in Browning in a M23 combination mount. In a postwar development it was fitted with the M24 Chaffee light tank turret, which mounted a 76mm gun.

Eight-wheeled Armored Cars

The Christie-designed tanks had always been intended to run on roads, using their roadwheels and only needing to fit tracks when travelling cross-country. Thus it was only logical to design an

armored car, which had the same number of wheels (four on each side) as the Christie-type medium tanks, because the wheels would make the vehicle faster, quieter and require less maintenance. This led to the trackless tank being designed by the Trackless Tank Corporation in 1940 and tested at the Aberdeen Proving Ground (APG), Maryland the following year. Powered by a 270hp Guiberson diesel engine, and a five-speed manual transmission, it had chain drive to the three rear axles and steering only to the front axle. Only one was ever built.

Using all the experience gained from the trackless tank project the 14.3ton, T13 armored

Above: **The T18 HMC, (Howitzer Motor Carriage) mounted a 75mm howitzer in a massive cast hull on a M3 light tank chassis.** *(TM)*

Top: **The T18E2 Boarhound armored car of 1942 followed on from the T18 pilot model. Built for the British but only thirty were ever completed.** *(TM)*

car was built in prototype form by the Reo Company in 1941. It had welded armor, mounted a 37mm main gun and co-ax .30in MG in the turret and had another MG in the hull. Three only were built and its dimensions were 17ft 1in long, 8ft 4ins wide and 7ft 2ins high.

The Yellow Coach division of General Motors built the T18 a large – over 26 tons – armored car in 1942. It led directly on to the T18E2, known by the British as the Boarhound.

Very heavy at 26.8 tons and very large – 20ft 6ins long, 10ft 1in wide and 8ft 7ins high – it mounted a formidable 57mm (6 pounder) gun, plus two machine guns (as for the T13). Armor thickness was up to 50mm in some parts. Thirty were built for the British, but never saw action. One remains at the Tank Museum, Bovington.

Built by Studebaker, the T27 armored car of 1943 was a good looking vehicle, which resembled the Greyhound, but had eight equally

spaced wheels and individual cupolas for the driver and co-driver. Weighing only 7.5tons fully stowed it could cruise at 60mph and had armor up to 20mm thick. The 8x6 four-man T27 was 17ft 1½in long, 7ft 6½ins wide and 6ft 6½ins high.

The T55 3-inch GMC of 1942 was an enormous wheeled chassis similar to the T18, but mounted a 3-inch gun to the right of the driver in an open-topped hull. A .50in machine gun

was located in the rear deck of the hull. Also known as 'Cook's Cozy Cabin', it was 25ft 7½ins long (including the gun), 9ft 3½ins wide and 8ft 9½ins high.

Carriers

The T16 carrier universal was manufactured in America, by the Ford Motor Company of Somerville, Massachusetts, which was the only plant in the United States to produce the vehicle. After preliminary negotiations with the American and British Governments, Ford engineers carried out detailed testing on the Universal Carrier, then redesigned it with two aims. Firstly to improve performance and secondly to simplify the design so that it could be more easily and quickly manufactured. It was then agreed that 21,000 would be built, Ford accepting a letter of intent from US Army Ordnance on 30 September 1942. Production followed some months later, in March 1943, reaching a peak in June 1944 when 1,040 were completed and reducing in May 1945 when the final 122 were finished. In between those dates, the production total was reduced, so that in the end only 13,893 T16s were completed. The

Above: **The T55 GMC, also known as 'Cook's Cozy Cabin', was over 25ft long and mounted a 3-inch gun in an open-topped hull on a T18 chassis.** *(TM)*

Far left: **The T27 armored car was built by Studebaker, in 1943. It weighed only 7.5 tons and cruised at over 60mph.** *(TM)*

Left centre: **M 29 Weasels on trials in muddy pool adjacent to the Ford factory.** *(TM)*

Right: **US Marine Corps Weasel carrying a full load of refugees. Okinowa, 1945.** *(TM)*

Below: **A standard production Ford T16 Universal Carrier.** *(GF)*

Bottom: **Weasel fitted with flamethrower equipment, making it a highly lethal weapon.** *(TM)*

main reason for this reduction was that the war in Europe was clearly ending and the M28/M29 Weasel cargo carrier was considered more suitable in the fighting against Japan. Ford then switched to the production of the Weasel.

Ford's survey had found that the British T16 was of riveted construction, which they considered would not stand up to the battlefield conditions expected, therefore they chose a welded hull which was not only stronger and waterproof, but was also capable of being manufactured more efficiently and economically. The redesigned carrier was a righthand drive, fully-tracked vehicle, powered by a 100hp Ford engine and was operated by two steering levers directly in front of the driver. It had four forward gears and reverse. A number of T16s produced were equipped with radio (WS 19) and Intraphone. It had four bogie wheels on each side, instead of three. Specifications for the Universal Carrier T16 as it was now called were: Battle Weight: 4.21 tons (empty the T16 weighed 3.46 ton) Crew four, length 12ft 8½ins, width 6ft 11ins and height 5ft½in, Engine: V8 100hp Ford- Mercury,

located lengthwise, in the centre of the hull. A Mk II was produced in 1945, on which the positions of the bogie wheels were altered slightly in order to give better stability.

Having carried out operations in both Alaska and the Aleutians, the need for a special tracked vehicle which could easily move over snow became apparent. In 1943, the M28 Carrier named Weasel entered service. Weighing only 2.68 tons it carried a crew of two to four men and had tracks eighteen inches wide, so its performance on snow was excellent. It had a limited cargo capacity of 1,200lb, but could tow 4,200lb. It was powered by a rear-mounted six-cylinder 65hp Studebaker engine, with drive sprockets at the front and had a range of approximately 175 miles. It was followed rapidly by the M29, which had the engine in front and drive sprockets at the rear, this improved the performance and gave more space for stowage. Tracks were also widened by two inches to twenty inches. A third model, the M29C was also produced which was fully amphibious with buoyancy chambers, twin rudders and a spray guard on the bow. Weasel was

Left: **A fully amphibious M29C Weasel, fitted with twin rudders and spray guard.** *(TM)*

Right: **An M8 HMC in action. Between September 1942 and January 1944, Cadillac built 1,778 of these excellent 75mm self-propelled howitzers. All were built on the M5 light tank chassis.** *(TM)*

especially useful in such places as the mountains of Italy, where the US Army 10th Mountain Division was operating. Dimensions of this excellent little vehicle were: length: 16ft, width: 5ft 7½ins and height: 5ft 11ins.

Although ideal in snow it also performed well in other conditions and, as explained was selected for use against the Japanese. Ford Motor Company of Somerville signed a contract in January 1945 to produce 10,692, did its engi-

neering work and prepared the factory ready for production, just as the war ended!

Self-propelled Artillery

As with the Germans, the Americans enthusiastically embraced the building of a vast number of self-propelled guns and howitzers, but many models never proceded further than the prototype

Right: **The M37 (T 76) 105 mm HMC was designed and built on the Chaffee light tank chassis to replace the M7 HMC, but only a few were completed before the end of World War Two.** *(TM)*

Left: **A well restored White M3A1 scout car photographed at one of the Tank Museum's AFV rallies. Note the sprung roller front bumper.** *(TM/Roland Groom)*

Below: **On the Bovington Training Area during one of the RAC Centre's 'Battle Days' is this well equipped and restored White half-track, armed with both .50in and .30in Browning machine guns.** *(TM/Roland Groom)*

Right: **Another view of the Priest, showing four of the seven-man crew and the pulpit-mounted .50in Browning heavy machine gun.** *(Patton Museum)*

Left: **A privately-owned (part of the AF Budge Colleciton) M7 Priest HMC, mounted a 105mm howitzer. It became the standard equipment of artillery battalions in US Armored Divisions.**
(TM/Roland Groom)

Left: **This M7 HMC was in service with a Free French SP artillery regiment. The Americans provided most of the equipment for the French 2nd Armoured Division, which was part of General Patton's Third Army.**
(TM)

Right: **An M20 Utility Car restored by Roy Halsall. Nearly 4,000 of these extremely useful AFVs were built.** *(TM/Roland Groom)*

Below: **The M20 was a turretless M8 Greyhound, armed with a ring-mounted .50in Browning heavy machine gun.** *(TM/Roland Groom)*

Below centre: **The only remaining T16E2 Boarhound armoured car in Great Britain is at the Tank Museum. It was a massive 26.8 ton vehicle, armed with a 57mm gun.**
(TM/Roland Groom)

Below: **The M8 Greyhound was the only armoured car to be used by the US Army in large numbers. Over 8.500 were built by the Ford Motor Company.**
(TM/Roland Groom)

Right: **The GMC M10 tank destroyer, mounted an M7 gun, was also known as the Wolverine. This one, in service with the US First Army is seen passing through the damaged town of Duren, Germany in February 1945. It is still fitted with a Culin hedgerow cutter which had proved invaluable in the *bocage* countryside of Normandy.** *(TM)*

Right: **Snow camouflaged and bearing the 11th Armoured Division's black bull insignia, this M10 Achilles mounted the excellent British 17 pounder gun.** *(TM/Roland Groom)*

Below: **M10s were sometimes used to provide artillery support, especially when there were shortages of conventional artillery. The 3-inch gun had a maximum range in excess of 14,500metres and fifty-four rounds were carried on the vehicle.** *(TM)*

Right: **The diminutive 2.68 ton Weasel tracked carrier was originally introduced for use over snow. 'Grumpy' was one of two privately-owned Weasels on display at the 50th anniversary of the Victory in Europe Military Vehicle Show, Southsea, England in 1995.** *(TM/Roland Groom)*

Below: **And this is the other! The excellent M28/29 Weasel could carry a 1,200lbs load or tow a weight of 4,200lbs. It was widely used in all theatres.** *(TM/Roland Groom)*

Above: **Standard equipment for all artillery battalions of American armored divisions. The M7 and M7B1, mounted a 105mm howitzer on M3 or M4A3 medium tank chassis. They were known as Priest in the British service.** *(TM)*

stage, being built either as 'one-offs' or in just sufficient quantity for thorough testing, but then never entering service. An approximate count of 'T' & 'M' numbered Gun Motor Carriages, Howitzer Motor Carriages, Multiple Gun Motor Carriages, Mortar Motor Carriages, Rocket Projectors and Flamethrowers, mounted on tracked, halftracked or wheeled chassis, adds up to well over two hundred different items, although of course a number of Ts did result in Ms. In my book on *World War Two Tanks* in this series I have mentioned some of the rocket projectors and flamethrowers, but that only reduces the list by around forty. Of necessity, I must limit our examination to the more important SPs amongst those of the first four types (Guns, Howitzers, Multiple Guns and Mortars) most of which saw operational service and were mounted on tank chassis.

Smallest of the tank mounted SPs was the Howitzer Motor Carriage (HMC) M8 of 1942. This used the M5 light tank chassis on which was mounted a 75mm Pack howitzer, already successfully fitted on a M3 halftrack. The first attempt had a large open-topped superstructure, with the howitzer mounted in the hull front, resembling the M7, but it lacked crew protection and was replaced by a much better designed open-topped turret which fitted on the existing tank's turret ring. Cadillac built a total of 1,778 M8s, between September 1942 and January 1944, which were widely used in both the European and Pacific theatres, by the

headquarters companies of medium tank battalions. One major drawback was the small ammunition load carried – only forty-six rounds (compare with sixty-nine on the M7), so it was fitted with a towing hook to pull an ammunition trailer.

M8 HMC

Specification	
Weight (tons)	15.4 (fully stowed)
Dimensions	
Length:	14ft 6ins
Width:	7ft 4^1/$_2$ins
Height:	7ft 7^1/$_2$ins
Crew:	four
Engine:	twin V8 110hp Cadillac petrol
Armor:	10-28mm
Armament:	75mm Howitzer M2 & M3
	(elevation minus 20 degrees to plus 40
	degrees. Traverse 360 degrees)
Top speed:	35mph
Range	130miles

Although the HMC M37 was designed and built to replace the M7, only a few were produced before the war ended. It was based on the M24 Chaffee light tank and mounted a 105mm M4 howitzer. Not only did it mount a larger howitzer with better elevation, so that its range was greatly increased, but it was also able to carry ninety rounds of ammunition. Total build was eventually 316.

Plans to mount a 105mm howitzer on the M3 medium tank chassis began in mid-1941, in order to provide self-propelled artillery for the US Army's armored divisions. Two T32 pilot models were built, both mounted the 105mm M1A2 howitzer in an open-topped superstructure, which permitted only limited traverse (fifteen degrees left to thirty degrees right) and elevation from minus five degrees to plus thirty-five degrees. Secondary AA armament was a .50in heavy machine gun in the raised commander's station, known as the 'pulpit'. Standardised as the M7 HMC, over 2,000 were built by American Locomotive in 1942 and just over 3,000 in total were built by the end of the war (American Locomotive – 2,208; Pressed Steel – 826; Federal Walker – 127).

The HMC M7 was inspected by the British Tank Mission in early 1942 and a request was immediately placed for 2,500 with delivery by the end of 1942 plus a further 3,000 in 1943. Clearly supply could never meet demand, although ninety were sent to North Africa in the early autumn of 1942 for the British 8th Army, just as M3 light and M3 medium tanks had been sent earlier that year. The British designated M7 as the 105mm SP Priest, and they were later used to equip some of the mobile artillery units in British armored divisions deployed to Normandy in June 1944, but these were soon replaced by Canadian-built Sextons.

In 1943, production of the M4 Sherman took over from the M3, so the M7 was replaced by the M7B1 and M7B2, both based on the chassis of the M4A3, the M7B2 having a higher pulpit and other minor changes. Variants included:

PRIEST KANGAROO APC. A total of 102 Priests were stripped-out by the British for use as APCs. These could carry twenty fully-equipped infantrymen as well as the two crewmen (commander and driver). All this work was carried out in the field by a number of different armored brigade workshops in Italy, between October 1944 and the end of the war.

PRIEST OP. A Priest with the 105mm gun and other equipment removed to make room for all the extra radios, field telephones, cable drums and other items needed by FOOs (Forward Observation Officers).

M7 HMC

Specification	
Weight (tons)	22.6 (the M7B1 was 650lb lighter)
Dimensions	
Length:	19ft 9ins
Width:	9ft 5³/₄ins
Height:	8ft 4ins
Crew:	Seven (five gun crew, plus commander and driver)
Engine:	M7 - Wright Continental R-975 air-cooled radial; M7B1 & M7B2 - V8 Ford GAA petrol
Armament:	105mm howitzer M1A2, M2 & M2A1 (traverse 15 degrees left, 30 degrees right. Elevation minus five degrees to plus thirty-five degrees)
Armor:	12-62mm
Top speed:	25mph
Range:	125 miles

Development of a 155mm SP gun on the M3 medium tank chassis was first suggested in June 1941, the pilot model – GMC T6 was produced in early 1942, tested and rejected. Ordnance, however, considered it to be superior to the towed 155mm gun and requested a build of fifty for further testing, but this was overruled by the Supply Department pending a full test by the Artillery Board. When this proved successful, Supply were overruled and the SP was designated GMC M12 and an order placed for 100 to be built. This build was completed in March 1943, but the vehicles were not issued opera-

tionally, but used instead for training in the United States until late 1943, when seventy-five were overhauled for use in the coming invasion. They were dispatched to the European Theatre of Operations (ETO) in June 1944 and took part in several major actions which included the capture of Cologne in March 1945. One variant was produced the M30 cargo carrier, which was identical to the M12, but without the gun and recoil spade at the rear. It was used to carry extra gun crew and ammunition (forty rounds) as the SP only carried ten rounds.

M12 GMC

Specification	
Weight (tons)	25.9 (the M30 was 4.9 tons lighter)
Dimensions	
Length	22ft 1in
Width:	8ft 9ins
Height:	8ft 10ins
Crew:	six (including four gun crew)
Engine:	353hp Wright Continental R-975 air-cooled radial
Armor:	10-50mm
Armament:	155mm M1918M1 gun, (traverse fourteen degrees either side of centre and elevation from minus five degrees to plus thirty degrees)
Max speed:	12mph
Range:	140 miles

The decision to overhaul the GMC M12 and its subsequent success in action had raised a call

Above: **A 155 mm M12 GMC being prepared for action in Belgium, 1944. The Cargo variant, to supply the M12 GMC, had the 155 mm gun removed to make space for ammunition.** *(TM)*

from the Armored Force for more heavy, tracked artillery to be made available. This and other tactical decisions had led to work being undertaken on a series of vehicles to be known under the generic title of the 'medium weight combat team' and based on the Sherman M4A3 chassis. A new 155mm gun was projected for this series and work began on two pilots in March 1944, the designation being T83.

The M4A3E8 chassis, which was fitted with the latest Horizontal Volute Spring Suspension (HVSS) as opposed to the older Vertical Volute (VVSS), had to be strengthened and widened slightly. It was designed from the outset so that the mount would allow the 8-inch howitzer to be fitted in place of the 155mm gun. At the same time, a cargo carrier was designed on the same chassis (without gun and mount) to carry spare crew and extra ammunition. After the D-Day landings, a build of just over 300 of each was authorised and began in early 1945 at the Pressed Steel factory, Pittsburgh. Standardised as the GMC M40, it earned the nickname 'Long Tom', because of the length of the 155mm gun. The first two guns to arrive in Europe saw action in the bombardment of Cologne alongside GMC M12s. The number required was raised to 600, but only just over half were completed by the time the war ended.

Building the 8-inch howitzer variant was also authorised in August 1944, the last few pilot T83s being fitted with this gun in place of the 155mm. However, it was not standardised as the HMC M43 until after the war. There was also a proposal to mount a massive 250mm (10-inch) mortar on the same chassis and a mock-up of one was built being designated T94, but the war ended before this work was completed and the project was cancelled.

M40 GMC & M43 HMC

Specifications	
Weight (tons)	35.7
Dimensions	
Length:	20ft 7ins (howitzer) 29ft 9ins (gun)
Width:	10ft 4ins
Heigth:	8ft 9$\frac{1}{2}$ins
Crew:	eight (including six gun crew)
Engine:	395hp Wright Continental R-975 air-cooled radial
Armament:	8-inch howitzer or 155mm gun
Top speed:	24mph
Range:	105miles

A 'heavyweight combat team' was also proposed in early 1945, to be based on the T26 Pershing tank chassis and two heavy bombardment artillery types were planned. It was decided that the two weapons to be used would be the 240mm howitzer and the 8-inch gun. Pilot models were built by the Chrysler Corporation and designated as HMC T92 and GMC T93 respectively and both were ready for trials in 1945. It was decided to test them in battle and both were prepared for shipping to the Pacific for use in the invasion of Japan. However, the end of the war came and all orders were cancelled.

Tank Destroyers

German Blitzkrieg success in 1940 and 1941 prompted the Americans to urgently look for a new way of knocking-out tanks. At the time it was not considered that a tank was the best anti-tank weapon, instead the War Department felt that the answer was for a fast moving, highly mobile, very powerful new vehicle with the primary task of seeking out and destroying enemy tanks. This mobile anti-tank gun theory gave rise directly to the formation of the Tank Destroyer Command and, unfortunately, also hindered the programme to produce a more powerful tank to replace the M4 Sherman. The name Tank Destroyer (TD) was deliberately chosen to emphasise the aggressive role of the new anti-tank units.

The TD Centre was set up on 1 December 1941 at Fort Meade, Maryland but was later moved to Fort Hood, Texas in February 1942. By late 1942 the TD force was nearly 100,000 strong with eighty active units and a further sixty-four planned. Peak numbers were reached in early 1943, when there were 106 active TD battalions - only thirteen less than the total number of tank battalions! From then on the size of the TD force declined, principally because the enemy never used the massed armored formations against the Americans, as were seen on the Eastern Front. Also, serious casualties led to TD personnel having to be used as replacement tank crews, so that by March 1945 there were only sixty-eight TD battalions remaining. Nevertheless, they were courageous, capable fighters, fully living up to their motto: *Seek, Strike and Destroy.*

The ideal weapon for the TD force had to be a choice between a towed anti-tank gun or an SP, the eventual solution being a compromise, so that TD battalions contained equal numbers of each. There were three basic types of self-propelled TD: M10 Wolverine, M18 Hellcat and M36.

Specifications	M10	M18	M36
Weight (tons):	29.11	17.86	28.12
Crew:	all had five (commander, driver and three gun crew)		
Dimensions			
Length:	22ft 5ins★a (gun forward)	21ft 10ins	24ft 6ins
Width:	10ft	9ft 9ins	10ft
Height:	9ft 6ins (over top of AA MG mount)	8ft 5ins	10ft 9ins
Main Armament:	3-inch gun/ 17 pounder	76mm gun	90mm gun
Secondary:	.30in AA MG★b	.50in AA HMG	
Armor:	12-37mm	7-12mm	12-50mm
Engine:	Twin GMC 6-71 diesels★c	Continental R-975 or C4 (400hp) petrol	V8 Ford GAA petrol
Max speed:	30mph	50-55mph	26-30mph
Range:	200miles	150miles	150miles

Notes:

a. 23ft 10ins for M10 Achilles with 17 pounder gun.
b. also 2-inch mortar on Achilles.
c. V8 Ford GAA petrol on M10A1

Below: **M8 Hellcat – 'a tanker's dream' – was light, fast and fitted with the 76mm gun. This one is crossing the Moselle River in Germany, March 1945.** *(TM)*

The M10 Wolverine was based on the M3 medium tank (Lee/Grant) hull, with a 3-inch gun mounted in place of the existing 37mm turret and 75mm in the side sponson. The first model, known as the T24, proved to be both too tall and too complicated so it was cancelled in March 1942 and followed swiftly by the T40. This mounted a 3-inch AA gun in a low-angle mounting on the same chassis. The Tank Destroyers Command accepted this model, although it lacked speed and mobility. Standardised as the GMC M9, fifty were ordered. However, only twenty-nine of the required gun barrels could be found, so the project dragged on inconclusively and was finally cancelled in August 1942.

It was overtaken by the T35, which mounted a 3-inch gun on a Sherman M4A2 chassis, later replaced by an improved model the T35E1. This TD had a much lower silhouette, an angled hull, a five-sided open-topped turret and thinner armor allowing increased speed and mobility. Standardised as the GMC M10 in June 1942, demand was such that the Sherman M4A3 chassis had also to be used – known as the M10A1. Rushed to North Africa in early 1943, the M10 quickly replaced the GMC M3 (75mm gun on a halftrack) as the main weapon

of the tank destroyer battalions. It first saw action in mid-March 1943, near Maknassy in Tunisia. A total of 4,993 M10s and 1,713 M10A1s were built, of which 1,648 were supplied to the British Army and were used operationally in both France and Italy. From late 1944, the British started converting many of them by replacing the 3-inch gun with their own more powerful 17pounder. The resulting TD was known as the 17pounder Achilles, the Mk IC being from the M10 and the Mk IIC from the M10A1.

The M18 Hellcat, was designed as a tank destroyer from the outset rather than being an adaptation on a tank chassis. It owes its origin to the original US War Department requirement of December 1941 for a very fast, lightly armored, tracked vehicle, with a low silhouette and a powerful gun. Two pilots were built (using the already proven Christie-type fast tank suspension) mounting a 37mm anti-tank gun. The first was completed by mid-1942 and designated as the T49. After testing in July 1942, the TD Command asked for a more powerful gun to be fitted, namely the 75mm M3 as in the M4 Sherman. This however was fortunately substituted by the more powerful 76mm gun. Further development also brought the adoption of the nine-cylinder Wright R-975 air-cooled radial engine and torsion bar suspension in place of the Christie-type.

The result was the T70, which proved to be ideal and, after trials and a few small modifications, production began at the Buick factory in July 1943. The T70 was standardised as the M18 in February 1944 and a total of 2,507 were built up to October 1944 when production ceased. It was well liked by crews, who used it successfully in North West Europe and Italy, knocking out many enemy tanks. A crew member from one told the author – 'the Hellcat overcame many of the problems of the M10. It was lighter and far more mobile. Speed was much better. The 76mm was a good gun although it did not carry the impact power at a distance as the 3inch did, but we were able to sustain more rapid fire than we could with the M10'. Another simply described the Hellcat as being: 'a tanker's dream'.

M10A1s which had been sent back for maintenance from operational service.

Standardised in July 1944 as the GMC 36, they
were first used in action in France, August 1944.
Demand for the new TD increased after the
Normandy battles had shown that the 90mm was
undoubtedly the best US Army anti-tank weapon
to use against the heavier Panthers and Tigers.
Various expedients had to be employed to meet
orders, such as using the standard hulls of Sherman
M4A3s (known as the M36B1) and using M10
hulls (known as the M36B2). A total of 2,324 of all
models were produced.

Last of the trio was the heavily armed M36,
which owed its greater firepower to a decision
made in October 1942, to discover if the 90mm
AA gun could be adapted to the anti-tank rôle
in order to deal with the heavier enemy armor
which was then starting to appear on the battlefield. Early tests with the M10 showed that,
whilst the gun could be fitted satisfactorily, its
increased length and weight caused considerable problems. Test firings proved satisfactory,
but it was clear that a new turret was needed.
Two pilot models were built by Ford in March
1943 based on the M10A1 chassis. They were
completed that September and proved very successful, being given the designation GMC T71,
and an order placed for 500 vehicles.

Unfortunately only 300 hulls were available,
so the numbers had to be made up by using

Landing Vehicles Tracked (Armored)

The design of these vehicles owes much to the
prewar development work of Donald Roebling
Jr., who in the mid-1930s had designed a light-
weight tracked amphibian, called the Alligator,
for rescue work in the Florida Everglades. By
1940, Roebling had redesigned the vehicle to
suit US Marine Corps specifications and by
mid-1941 an order for the first 200 LVT1s was
placed. By August 1941, US Marine Corps
Tractor Battalions were forming to operate the
first of what later became a massive 18,000
LVTs of all types built during World War Two.
Of these 3,118 were LVT(Armored).

There were four models built during the war,
LVT(A)1 and LVT(A)2 were very similar, except

that the latter did not mount a 37mm gun nor have any decking, so that it could be used as an armored cargo carrier. It could carry up to 7,600lbs of freight, but this was normally limited to 4,100lbs. A total of 500 LVT(A)1s and 450 LVT(A)2s were built by Roebling and Ford.

The largest production run was of the next model, the LVT(A)4, nearly 1,900 being constructed. It mounted the turret of the HMC M8 which had a 75mm howitzer as its main weapon. The extra machine guns which had been present on the decking of the LVT(A) 1 and 2 were dispensed with to save weight. Highly successful, it lacked a powered gun traverse but this was

rectified on the LVT(A)5, designed in 1945. This last model did not enter service in time to be used operationally. Other armaments fitted included rocket launchers, flamethrowers and the turret from the M24 Chaffee which mounted a 76mm gun.

The US Marine Corps grouped their LVT(A)s into armored amphibian battalions while the US Army, who did the same, designated the LVT(A) as amphibious tanks. These battalions did sterling work in such tasks as beach assaults, beach defence and waterborne flank assaults, as well as both direct and indirect fire missions in which they fired many thousands of rounds.

Above: **The LVT(A)4 carried 100 ammunition rounds for the 75mm howitzer, exactly the same load as the M8 HMC. A total of 1,900 were built.** *(TM)*

Specifications				
Model	LVT(A)1	LVT(A)2	LVT(A)4	LVT(A)5
Weight (tons)	14.64	12.32 plus cargo	17.62	as for LVT(A)4
Crew	six	four	six	except fitted
Height	8ft 5ins	8ft 3ins	10ft 5ins	with powered
Armament	one 37mm gun	one .50in & one	one 75mm howitzer	gun traverse
	three .30in MG	.30in MGs	one .50in AA	
	(one co-ax)			
	one .50in AA			
Performance				
max land speed	25mph	20mph	20mph	
max water speed	6.5mph	7.5mph	7.5mph	
Range				
land	125miles	150miles	150miles	
water	75miles	50miles	75miles	

(NB: all were powered by a 250hp Continental W670-9A air-cooled petrol engine, and were 26ft 1in long, by 10ft 10ins wide and only varied in height as shown)

CHAPTER FIVE

Soviet Union

Besides unconventional scout vehicles like *Aerosans*, the Soviets also developed armoured cars during the war, though certainly not so vigorously as before the war.

Soviet Tanks and Combat Vehicles of World War Two by S J Zaloga and J Gradnsen.

Russia had shown an early interest in armoured cars even before World War One and this had continued during the Civil War. In the late 1920s to the early 1930s, once the car industry had been revitalised, the Red Army (RKKA – *Rabochiy Krestyanskaya Krasnaya Armiya*) began to show interest in new models. They classified armoured cars in two categories (like Germany); light – armed with machine guns, heavy – armed with 37mm to 45mm guns. Armoured cars were given the initials BA (*Bronieavtomobil* – armoured automobile), although sometimes the A was dropped. Their interest was not sustained during the war and by 1943-44, the Soviets were making less and less use of armoured cars, so as demand fell so did production. At the start of the Great Patriotic (World War Two), the RKKA had some 4,800 armoured cars in service, many in distant parts of the Soviet Union, such as their Far East. These were then gradually brought into action against the Germans, rather than the Soviets actually building many new ones. Virtually the only armoured car to be built during the latter half of the Great Patriotic War, was the small BA 64, which had very limited capabilities. They did, however, also produce an interesting range of light over snow fighting vehicles, known as *Aerosans*. In addition, they made use of limited numbers of British Universal Carriers, American M3 halftracks and M3 scout cars. They also of course, made major use of self-propelled artillery and rocket carriers (both wheeled and tracked), limited use of AA vehicles, tracked transporters for towing artillery guns and flamethrower tanks, together with other more specialised equipment such as armoured trains.

Armoured Cars

Early models, like the D-8 and D-12, produced in the 1920s were little more than GAZ-A automobiles (copies of imported Ford cars) fitted with some armour plate and two machine guns. The first purpose-built light armoured car was the FA-I of the 1930s, which had its machine gun in a proper turret. It was followed by the BA-20, which was still in service at the start of World War Two. The BA-20 was followed by the all-welded BA-20M, which had an aerial on the left side of the hull, in place of the frame aerial of the BA-20V. Later, they were joined in the 1930s by various prototype vehicles, made by other manufacturers. These included the 6x4 GAZ-TK, LB-NATI and the LB-62, however, none of them entered quantity production. They also included the BA-21, which was an attempt to mount a heavier body on the GAZ-21 6x4 lorry chassis, but was soon dropped. BA-20s and 20Ms were still in service when the war began, including one model specially adapted for railway use, the BA-20Sh.d (*Shelsnaya Doroga* – railway).

Above: **Soviet SU-76 self-propelled guns support Red Army infantry as they attack German positions at Koenigsberg, April 1945.** *(TM)*

Specifications			
Model	BA 20	BA-20M	BA-21
Weight (tons)	3.2	2.5	3.2
Crew	two	two	three
Dimensions			
Length:	12ft 2½ins	14ft 1½ins	14ft 11½ins
Width:	5ft 6ins	5ft 9ins	5ft 10ins
Height:	6ft 4ins	7ft 1in	7ft 1in
Armour		9–10mm	9–11mm
Armament	one 7.62mm DTMG		
Engine:	50hp four-cylinder GAZ-M1		
	water-cooled		
Top speed	47mph	55mph	33mph
Range	280miles	212miles	

The only new armoured car to be standardised by the Soviet Union was the BA-64 a small, two-man 2.36 ton scout car, powered by a 50hp four-cylinder GAZ-MM engine. Based on the GAZ-64 type jeep and designed mainly for liaison work, the two-man BA-64A car was also used for reconnaissance and other tasks. It was designed and produced by GAZ, but shows distinct German influences in its body shape and armour design. Dimensions were 12ft long, 5ft wide and 6ft 3ins high, the car had a top speed of 50mph and a range of 280 miles. When the GAZ-67B type jeep entered service, the BA-64B became the production model, the main difference being that the 7.62mm machine gun was now mounted in a small turret rather

than being pintle mounted at the front of the open top. Variants included:

BA 64 with DShK 1938 MG.– a model which mounted a 12.7mm heavy machine gun on top of the scout car's existing open-topped turret. It was built in small numbers during 1944.

BA 64 D – airborne/raiding version on which the turret was completely removed, so that it could carry up to six men – it never entered production.

There were also halftrack and rail versions of this well-liked diminutive vehicle which was affectionately known as *Bobik* by its crews. Total wartime production was about 3,500.

Heavy Armoured Cars

Among the first armoured cars to be built after the start of the first Five-Year Plan in 1927, was the 4.5ton BA-27 which had rivetted armour, a crew of two and mounted a 37mm gun and a co-ax MG. It was followed in the 1930s by the BA-1, BA-3 and BA-6. The first of the three was based on an imported Ford-Timken lorry chassis, but it did not enter production because the new GAZ-AAA lorry chassis became available and this formed the basis of the BA-3. It used the turret of the T-26 light tank, mounting a 45mm gun, but proved to be too heavy so production was halted. Instead, the BA-6 was designed, which had a lightened armoured body (nearly 2240lbs lighter), better suspension and

Right: **German soldiers inspect a captured BA-20Sh.d, which was the BA-20 four-wheeled armoured car, adapted for railway use.** *(TM)*

Below right: **Mass parade of BA-20Vs. This was the commander's version of the BA-20 armoured car. Note the large frame aerial around the top of the body.** *(TM)*

Below: **The only new scout/ armoured car built by the Russians in World War Two was the diminutive 2.36 ton BA-64. This one is at the Russian War Museum in Moscow.** *(TM)*

transmission. As with the BA-20 a modernised version, designated BA-6M, was later produced also a rail version, the BA-6Sh.d. In 1936, the BA-6M was fully modernised, the new armoured car being known as the BA-10. It had the same hull and six-wheel suspension as the other earlier models, but mounted a 45mm semi-automatic gun in the T-30 experimental light tank turret, together with a co-ax MG, plus another machine gun in the hull next to the driver. The 5.2 ton BA-10 had armour up to 10mm thick, a four-man crew (two in the turret), a top speed of 53mph and a range of 185 miles.

In 1937, the BA-10M appeared which had a welded hull and was slightly heavier (5.3 tons). It measured 15ft 5ins long, and 6ft 10¾ins

wide, by 7ft 11¼ins high. Its armour was 11–14mm thick and power came from an 85hp GAZ M1 engine, giving it a top speed of 54mph and a range of 200miles. BA-6s and BA-10s both saw active service during the war, some being stripped-out for use as armoured personnel carriers. Others were delivered to China for use in their war against the Japanese. In common with the other Soviet armoured cars, track bands were carried, which could be slipped over the rear wheels to improve cross-country performance.

The BAZ amphibian (*Amfibyi*) version of the BA-6 was produced in the 1930s, using the GAZ-AAA lorry chassis to carry a distinctive boat-shaped hull. The fully-traversing turret mounted a 37mm gun also there were two large sponson-type turrets – one beside the driver's position, which itself had a large cover eighteen inches tall, and one behind the main turret. Each sponson contained a machine gun. The four-man crew was made up of commander (who also loaded and fired the 37mm gun), two machine gunners (each in a separate sponson-type turret) and the driver. While the front sponson was fixed, the rear-mounted one was capable of rotating through 270 degrees. The 7ton BAZ, had two brass propellers for water propulsion (6.5mph in water) and a rudder for steering, as well as its six road wheels. Dimensions were: 21ft 3½ins long, 6ft 11ins wide and 7ft 2½ins high. The BAZ did suffer from the same problem of exiting (up slippery river banks) as all-wheeled amphibians.

Above: **Amid the smoke of battle, a six-wheeled BA-10 heavy armoured car, with its turret traversed to the rear, drives in front of a massive KV 2 heavy tank. The spare wheel on the side of the BA-10 is almost grounded.** *(TM)*

Left: **The BAZ amphibious armoured car had a distinctive boat-shaped hull and mounted a 37mm gun, plus two MGs.** *(TM)*

Aerosans

The earliest of these *Aerosans* light sled-type vehicles, first deployed in the Winter War

against Finland (November 1939 to March 1940), were only constructed from plywood and powered by obsolete aeroplane engines. They were used for moving vital supplies over deep snow, which was impassable to normal wheeled or tracked vehicles. Some of the OSGA-6 (also known as the NKL-6) and KM-5 *Aerosans* were also used, fitted with a roof-mounted machine gun on a ring mount to support raiding parties (four or five men on the sled and four more towed behind on skis). Later, improved versions, known as NKL-16/41 and 16/42 were produced and these led on to the production of an armoured

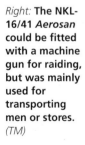

Right: **The NKL-16/41 *Aerosan* could be fitted with a machine gun for raiding, but was mainly used for transporting men or stores.** *(TM)*

Self-propelled Artillery

From 1942 onwards, the Red Army produced a comprehensive range of SP assault guns and achieved major success, taking note of what the Germans had done, by keeping the number of different models to a minimum. They had begun development of SP artillery much earlier of course, in the 1930s, using tank chassis to mount a number of different weapons, ranging from 37mm anti-tank guns to 152mm ex-naval guns and even larger calibre howitzers. However, the muddled thinking of men like General Pavlov, combined with Stalin's savage purge of his real tank experts like Tukhachevsky, held back all development. It was not until the formation of the new tank and mechanised corps from 1942, that the desperate need for mechanised artillery to support them was fully realised.

In fact, designing the first of these new mechanised guns had already begun as the armoured forces themselves had grown tired of the painfully slow progress being made by the Directorate of Artillery towards mechanisation – caused in part, it has to be said, by the unreliability of many of the early means of mechanising the guns. In early 1942, development work had started on a light self-propelled gun using the T-60 light tank chassis and mounting the standard 76.2mm ZiS-3 divisional gun. It was called OSU-76 (*Opytnaya Samokhodnaya Ustanokva* – experimental mechanised mounting). The chassis was found to be too small, so work was transferred to the larger T-70 chassis. By moving the driver, engines and fuel tanks all to the front, it was possible to mount the gun on a slightly lengthened chassis,

version, the NKL-26 armoured *Aerosan*, with 10mm armoured plate on the nose. Organised into battalions, with forty-five *Aerosans* divided into three companies, they were used mainly in the north on flat ground (over frozen lakes and rivers) as the sled had difficulty ascending hills.

at the rear in a simple open-topped, box-shaped hull. Standardised as the SU-76 the first twenty-six were built in 1942. They were not a success, proving to be as unreliable as the early T-70 tank. This was mainly because of the engine arrangement, so it was decided to follow the same configuration as the T-70M, which had the two engines in line. Some hull modifications were necessary and the improved SU-76M started to roll off the assembly lines in large numbers. It had only mediocre success in the anti-tank rôle, not only because the Germans started to use better armoured tanks, but also because the effective range of the SU-76 was greatly reduced when firing AP ammunition. In the infantry support artillery rôle, where it could use the over 11,000 metres range of the gun to full advantage, it performed much better. However, it was not liked by the crews, because of the lack of overhead protection. They called it *Suka* (Bitch). A version with better all-round protection was produced, the SU-76B, but this proved to be far too heavy and was not accepted into service. The gun could fire four types of ammunition: HE, APHE, HVAP and HEAT. Sixty rounds of ammunition were carried and the vehicle measured 16ft 8½ins long, 9ft 1¾ins wide and 7ft high.

In mid-1942, work commenced on designing the fitting of the 122mm M-38 field howitzer on the T-34 chassis, with all-round armoured protection. Everything went according to plan and the first SU-122 rolled off the assembly line at the end of 1942. It went into action in January 1943. From the outset it was not considered as an anti-tank weapon, the anti-tank HEAT ammunition round proving to be a disappointment. They even went as far as to produce a longer barrelled version (SU-122P),

but this proved to be too long for the chassis and never entered production. So, it remained an infantry assault gun for direct fire support against defended localities.

Another dual purpose weapon was the SU-152, which mounted a massive 152 mm howitzer on a KV-1 chassis. It did exceptionally well in the anti-tank rôle, earning the nickname *Zvierboy* (Animal Killer) as it could knock-out Tigers, Panthers and even Elefants. Twelve SU-152s were rushed to the Kursk battlefield, reinforced later with a further nine. It is rumoured that the SU-152s had been designed in less than a month.

Specifications				
Model	SU-122	SU-152	ISU-122	ISU-152
Weight(Tons)	31	45.5	45.5	46
Crew	all five			
Dimensions				
Length:	23ft 2ins	29ft 10ins	32ft 10ins	30ft 7ins
Width:	10ft	10ft 10ins	10ft 2½ins	10ft 2½ins
Height:	7ft 8½ins	8ft 2ins	8ft 3½ins	8ft 3½ins
Main Armament	122mm	152mm	122mm	152mm
Engine	all powered with V12 V-2 Type diesels			
	500hp		all 600 hp	
Top speed	35mph	27mph	23mph	23mph
Range miles	188	206	both	138

When production of the KV-1 tank ended in 1943, it was decided to use the IS-1 chassis as the basis for a new heavy assault gun, mounting the 152mm ML-20 howitzer. This gun had the advantage of using the same carriage and recuperator system as the 122mm A-19 gun, so it was possible to produce both an ISU-152 and an ISU-122, simply by changing barrels and re-organising internal ammunition

Left: **The ISU-152 heavy self-propelled gun entered service in 1944, and provided long-range covering fire to support attacking formations. It was normally used in the direct fire role.** *(TM)*

stowage. On both these models, the crew compartments were enlarged, being higher, with less sloping sides, while the KV-type hatches were replaced with IS-type cupolas. The ISU-122 mounted the M-1944 L/45 A-19 gun with a wedge breech block and fired a 55lb shell to a range of 13,000 metres. After a total of almost 2,500 had been produced the next series were fitted with the 122mm D-25S L/43 tank gun, with a large muzzle break, which had better armour penetration. The 152mm howitzer fired an HE shell weighing 96lb to a range of 8,960 metres and, despite its slow rate of fire, its 107lb AP round could start to kill enemy tanks at phenomenal ranges. The only drawback was the small ammunition load carried of only twenty rounds.

Artillery Tractors

Artillery tractors were somewhat neglected because of the pressing need to build tanks, the only one to be built in any quantity being the

Above: **Two ISU-122s (the one in front is without a muzzle brake) are part of a Red Army raiding party which crossed into Transylvania, October 1944.** *(TM)*

Right: **ZSU-37s in a parade on Red Square, Moscow. A small number were built between 1944 and 1945, but it was beset with problems due to poor turret traverse speed.** *(TM)*

Above: **In mid-1944 the SU-100 was one of the best tank destroyers in service but was vulnerable as it was not fitted with defensive machine guns.** *(TM)*

YA-12. This was based on the light tank series and designed to tow the 152mm howitzer. It was later re-engined.

SP Anti-tank Guns

Early in the war, two small self-propelled anti-tank guns were used, both were based on armoured conversions of the Komsomolets tractor. The first the SU-45, mounted a 45mm gun (as on the BT-7 tank) in an armoured box-like turret inside of which the crew could stand. It weighed 6tons, had a crew of three and carried forty rounds of ammunition. The tractor's diesel

engine (positioned at the front now instead of the normal rear position) gave it a top speed of 25mph and a range 156miles. The lighter 4-ton SU-57, mounted a larger gun, but had no crew protection apart from a gunshield. Its speed and range remained the same as the SU-45.

Tank Destroyers

Attempts to mount an 85mm anti-aircraft gun on the T-70 light tank chassis got no further than the prototype stage as the gun was too long for the chassis. The design team for the new SU-85 was headed by S N Machinowa and included L S Trajanowa, a celebrated woman engineer. The new vehicle was built at the Uramaisz i Celabinski factory, the first one hundred appearing at the end of 1943 on the Dneiper and Ukraine fronts.

In 1944, as German heavy tanks were now being met in ever-increasing numbers, it was decided to fit the more powerful 100mm gun, using the same chassis, the resulting SU-100 resembled the SU-85 in many ways, apart of course from armament. The well-sloped hull was of welded construction whilst the super-structure, housing the fighting compartment, had an angled front plate (including the glacis plate). The gun was offset to the right of cen-tre, with the commander's station behind.

There was a cupola, with a hinged hatch cover, plus a second hinged hatch in the roof to the left of the gun. The driver's position was on the left, with the gunner immediately behind him, while the loader stood at the rear of the fighting compartment.

Specifications	SU-85	SU-100
Weight (tons)	29.2	31.5
Crew	four	four
Dimensions		
Length :	27ft 2ins	31ft 6ins
Width:	10ft	10ft
Height:	8ft 4ins	7ft 6ins
Armament:	85mm gun	100mm gun
	D 5-S	D 10-S
Engine	(both) V12 500hp V-2 type	
	diesel engine	
Top speed	30mph	30mph
Range:	250miles	200miles

Tracked Anti-aircraft Vehicles

Despite significant armoured vehicles losses from air attack, the Soviets did not produce any really effective tracked AA guns, until well after the end of the war, when the ZSU-57-2 and ZSU-23-4 were developed in the 1950s. Instead, they depended on a mixture of lorry-mounted, light

AA weapons (quadruple Maxim MGs or a 37mm gun on a GAZ AA lorry) or on American equipment such as the M15 and M17 multiple GMC on an M3 halftrack chassis, over 1,000 of which had been supplied under lend-lease.

An attempt was made to use first the T-60 light tank chassis, then the T-70, to mount twin 12.7mm heavy machine guns, but this project was shelved in 1943, in favour of mounting a 37mm AA gun on a modified SU-76 chassis. The resulting ZSU-37 was beset with problems, in particular concerning the speed at which the gun could be traversed, and only a few hundred were produced.

Armoured Trains

By far the largest armoured fighting vehicles in the Red Army's arsenal were their armoured trains. Despite being vulnerable to attack from the air or from tanks, they were used on various occasions, mainly to provide fire support to the attacking infantry. During the battles for Stalingrad, eight armoured train battalions were in action. The trains were mainly armed with tank turrets from T-34 or KV-1, although there were some special armoured trains, mounting AA guns and MGs, to provide vital railway shipments with mobile, on the spot protection. There were also armoured artillery trains, which mounted even larger guns.

Above: **Armoured trains of the Red Army were heavily equipped with a variety of different gun turrets.** *(TM)*

CHAPTER SIX

France

Good, if somewhat old fashioned equipment, but used in an outdated way thanks to an all-pervading false sense of security.

The building of the Maginot Line had undoubtedly given France a sense of false security, nevertheless, just as the French Army had a reasonable number of good tanks in service in 1939, so also were they quite well equipped with armoured cars. Of the three types of French cavalry, the third the AMD – *Automitrailleuse de Decouverte* (long-range reconnaissace machine gun cars), was entirely the primary task of armoured cars, whilst armoured cars and halftracks were also to be found in the two other classifications of cavalry vehicles, *Automitrailleuses de Reconnaissance* (AMR) and *Automitrailleuses de Combat* (AMC), although they were mainly equipped with light and light medium tanks. In addition to those in Metropolitan France, some armoured cars and other AFVs were in North Africa, the Middle East and Far East, helping to maintain law and order in the French colonial empire. One source puts the figure at 200 armoured cars abroad. During the Blitzkrieg invasion of France in 1940, the French Army in mainland France had over 400 inter-war armoured cars in service, including about 350 of their latest Panhard AMD 178 in reconnaissance units.

After the defeat a number of French armoured cars, together with various other items of military hardware, were taken over by the Germans. Others were clandestinely 'acquired' by the French Resistance or even manufactured by them from stolen parts! This unfortunately ended when

a traitor informed on these covert operations. The Germans not only used the captured AFVs in their correct rôle, but also fitted them with other weapons – for example, mounting a 7.5cm PaK 40 anti-tank gun on the Lorraine carrier, was but one of a number of adaptations. A few French armoured vehicles also later saw action with the Free French in North Africa against both the Italians and the Germans.

The French had made considerable use of *artillerie d'assaut* in World War One, when 400 each of their Schneider and St Chamond (both mounting 75mm guns) *Char d'assaut* were built. There were plans in hand to mount larger calibre guns (194mm and 280mm) on the St Chamond chassis when the war ended in 1918. Progress thereafter was minimal, due mainly to opposition from the entrenched 'horse artillery', backed by the Commander-in-Chief, so that when World War Two began the only SP artillery in service with the French Army was a handful of experimental models and prototypes.

Armoured Cars

The White-Laffly AMD (also called Laffly 50 AM) was originally built and used in World War One and a number of these elderly four-wheeled armoured cars were modernised in the 1920s and 1930s, by having their hulls raised and pneumatic tyres fitted. The resulting

armoured car weighed 6.5 tons, had a crew of four and measured 18ft long, by 7ft 3ins wide and 9ft 4ins high. There were still nearly 100 in service in 1940. A command version was fitted with a large and cumbersome grid aerial, mounted on top and supported on masts at the front of the car and posts on the turret. The three turret posts went up to a slip ring, which allowed the aerial to be traversed, once the vehicle was stationary, so as to pick up the strongest signal. Some were thought to have been used in the fighting against the Germans in 1940.

In 1924, Panhard produced the 165/175, a conventional-looking four wheeled armoured car, with disc wheels, a round turret with a bevelled-in top, mounting machine guns front and rear. This was modernised two years later (AM Panhard de 20CV), some of which had a 37mm gun in place of one of the machine guns. The same turret was used on the Renault AM 20CV of the same period. In 1933, Panhard produced the AMD 165/175 which had a remodelled turret and larger wheels fitted with balloon tyres. It weighed 6.7 tons, had 9mm of armour, a top speed of 47mph and a range of 470 miles, whilst its dimensions were 18ft 2ins long, by 6ft 8½ins wide and 9ft 2ins high. It mounted a 37mm gun and co-ax MG in a faceted turret.

The next Panhard was the AMD 178, which appeared as a prototype in 1933. Known also as the AMD 35, it was the main successor to the White-Laffly and mounted a 25mm cannon and co-ax MG in a faceted turret. The 8.5 ton, four-wheeler had armour up to 20mm thick and was powered by an eight-cylinder Panhard engine which gave it a top speed of 45mph and a range of 187 miles. It had four-wheel drive and dual steering (for reverse driving). Dimensions were 15ft 11½ins long, by 6ft 8ins wide, by 7ft 8½ins high. The command version had the gun removed (but not the gun mounting) and the space occupied with larger radio sets. In total 529 were built by 1 June 1940. After World War Two it was fitted with a round, all-welded turret, mounting a 47mm gun and continued to be widely used by the French Army in Indo-China, Syria and elsewhere. As already mentioned, 350 were in service in France in May 1940 and it was undoubtedly the best armoured car in the French Army. The Germans made use of the ones they captured (nearly 200), designating it *Panzerspähwagen Panhard 178-P204(f)* and keeping the same armament.

In 1928, Laffly produced the 50 AMD, which had a centre-mounted Renault VM tank turret housing heavy and light machine guns. This was followed in 1931 by a number of prototypes for a series of armoured cars called the Laffly-Vincennes or AMD 80. The car finally went into production in 1934 and twenty-eight were constructed. It was still in use against the Germans and Italians in North Africa, 1942. Weighing 7.5 tons it had a top speed of 50mph and a range of 250miles. It had a crew of four

Above: **An AMD Panhard 178 here in German service in Russia when it was known as the** *Panzerspähwagen Panhard 178-P204(f).* **It was a good armoured car, weighing some 8.2 tons and mounting a 25 mm cannon.** *(TM)*

Right: **An improvised armoured car used by French Resistance fighters against the retreating Germans. The solid rubber tyres show that it was built on an early lorry chassis.** *(TM)*

Above: **Free French Forces locally modified commercial trucks into armoured vehicles. The one shown was used in Syria.** *(TM)*

and was armed with a 13.2mm heavy machine gun. Dimensions were: 19ft long, by 7ft wide, by 8ft 3½ins high. After the war, between 1945 and 1946, they were used in Algeria.

The Laffly S15 TOE AMD was a six-wheeled armoured car easily recognisable because of its small hemispherical turret on top of the body (not fitted on the prototype). Built in 1934, it weighed 5tons had a crew of three, mounted a single machine gun in the turret and was 15ft 2ins long, 6ft 2ins wide and 8ft 2ins high. It had a top speed of around 37mph and a range of 625 miles. It was also used as an armoured personnel carrier and to mount an artillery gun. Twenty-five were built and adapted for use in the heat and dust of North Africa.

Left: **An AMD Panhard 165/175 TOE, built in 1933, was a later model of the Panhard AM 20 CV, with armour 9 mm thick and weighing 6.7 tons.** *(TM)*

Below: **Side view of the AMD Panhard 165/175 TOE. Its chassis was 17ft 6ins long had a faceted turret and disc wheels.** *(TM)*

Above: **The Laffly-Vincennes, also known as the Laffly 80AM, was accepted into production in 1934. They were deployed during the war in North Africa and postwar in Algeria.** *(TM)*

Right: **This White-Laffly** *Automitrailleuse* **was rebuilt from First World War stock in 1925 with a raised hull and pneumatic tyres. This one was captured in North Africa, November 1942.** *(TM)*

Another company to produce armoured cars in the 1930s was Berliet, who built both 4x4 and 6x6 versions of their long-bodied armoured car which could also double as a small armoured personnel carrier, with room for a driver and seven men. Their 4x4 version, the VUDB (*Voiture de Prise de Contact*) was the most successful. Fifty were built and saw service in Metropolitan France, Morocco and a further twelve were purchased by Belgium. Another two 4x4s were the VUB of 1931-32 built for long range reconnaissance and the VUB B4 of 1932, built for close reconnaissance work (AMR) but after trials they were considered to be too large, too heavy and insufficiently armed.

Above: **Laffly S 15 TOE, the two nearest the camera being the command version with large aerial mountings fitted on the left front mudguard (only one has its antenna fitted), plus another on top of the small turret.** *(TM)*

Left: **The Laffly S 15 TOE, with the distinctive small hemispherical turret, weighed 5 tons and had a top speed of 37.5 mph. Note the small wheels at the front to help it negotiate obstacles.** *(TM)*

Right: **Fifty of these Berliet 4x4 VUDB were built for the French Army, then a further twelve for Belgium.
They saw service with the French in North Africa.** *(TM)*

Below: **The AMR 39, was the last of the Gendron-Somua prototypes, which mounted a 25mm gun and 7.5 mm co-ax in a well designed turret. It entered production in 1939.** *(TM)*

Left: **The Laffly S14 TOE was a prototype produced in 1934, which looked more like an APC than an armoured car – it could carry eight men.** *(TM)*

They also built two prototypes of a larger 6x6 vehicle, known as the VPRM, which was tested in France and Algeria but was not a success. Nevertheless, they persisted with the vehicle and in 1931 built a prototype of the ten-wheeled VPDM (the rear eight wheels being driven) specially constructed for the French Army in Morocco. This again was unsuccessful and was never put into production. Another Berliet model was the VUM (also called the *Automitrailleuse Syrie*) designed for service in Syria, but never progressed further than the prototype stage.

Gendron-Somua (also called Gendron-Poniatowski) was yet another series builder, beginning in 1934 and producing further models in 1935 and 1938. Finally in 1939 the production version of the Gendron-Somua AMR 39 appeared. It was an excellent-looking armoured car, weighing 3.8 tons, with a 25mm gun and co-ax MG in a well-shaped turret. The vehicle measured 17ft 4ins long, 7ft 2 $\frac{1}{2}$ins wide and 8ft 3ins high and it had a top speed of 43mph with a range of 250 miles. There is no record of it having entered service.

In addition to the above there were other four-wheeled armoured cars produced in the 1930s by Renault, Saurer (used in Morocco) and others. Also produced were six and eight-wheelers, even halftracks such as the Schneider AMC P16 and some Laffly APCs, but there is no hard evidence to say that all of them were used in action during World War Two. Presumably most of those stationed in mainland France during 1940 would have been deployed.

A number of improvised armoured cars were built by the French Resistance. These included the La Rochelle Mini and the La Rochelle, both made in 1945 using a motor car or lorry chassis fitted with locally manufactured armour plating and armoured machine guns.

Self-propelled Artillery

As already mentioned the French made practically no use of self-propelled artillery although

Below: **This version of the Laffly S15 had a 47mm gun mounted at the rear with gun shield and an armoured body.** *(TM)*

Right: **The Somua SAU 40 mounted a 75mm gun in the front of a cast hull, with a Char B turret offset to the left.** *(TM)*

Right: **Both the AMR 33 and AMR 35 were used to mount small calibre guns, this is the AMR 35 with a 25mm cannon. Note the small command cupola.** *(TM)*

there were some cases of mounting both anti-tank and artillery guns on six-wheeled Laffly trucks, some just being carried portée in the rear of the truck. There were only two examples of what could be termed wheeled SPs, the first and most important being the *L'autocanon de 75mm Modele 1913/1934*. This comprised a 75mm AA gun mounted on the rear of a wheeled chassis, (the gun had been developed before World War One, making it one of the very first AA guns, being designed for use against airships). It had been modernised in the early 1930s, but still had a very World War One appearance. A total of 236 were in service with fifty-seven AA batteries in May 1940. Several were captured by the Germans and some were still being used by them as late as 1944.

The second of wheeled SP, built in 1937, certainly looked a little more up to date. The Laffly *Chasseur du Char*, using the same chassis as the Laffly S15 TOE, mounted a 47mm SA/35 anti-tank gun on a rotating rear mount (270 degrees of traverse). It was ftted with an armoured windscreen, but unarmoured bonnet and cab. A later model of the *Chasseur du Char* used the same chassis but had an open-topped armoured box-like hull, with the gun only able to fire to the rear.

Work was in hand mounting anti-tank and artillery guns on various different tank chassis.

LIGHT TANKS – Both AMR 33 and AMR 35 were used to mount small calibre guns, the 33 a 37mm and the 35 a 25mm in the front of box-like fixed hulls, the AMR 35 having a small, raised cupola.

MEDIUM TANKS – SAU 40. This was the Somua S35 medium tank chassis with a 75mm gun mounted in the front of a streamlined box-like hull on top of which, offset to the left, was the S35 turret. After successful trials in 1939, an order was placed for thirty-six SAU 40, they were however, never built.

ARL – Produced at the same time as the SAU 40 and also mounting a 75mm gun this SP had a hull resembling that of the Char B, with the S35 turret in the centre. Only two were constructed and they were allegedly sent to North Africa during the débâcle of May 1940, but appear to have been lost without trace.

Halftracks

The Schneider AMC P16 (M 29) built in 1929 was a 6.8 ton halftrack, with a crew of three, a 37mm gun and one machine gun. It was 16ft 1in long, 5ft 9½ins wide and 8ft 8ins high. Armour was up 11.4mm thick and it had a top speed of 31mph and a range of 156 miles. Of the 100 built most were used mainly by cavalry regiments in France, but some were dispatched to Algeria. They were still in use in May 1940, equipping cavalry divisions along with Hotchkiss light tanks.

Carriers

Renault's Type UE (*Chenillette d'infanterie* – infantry carrier) was undoubtedly inspired by the Carden-Loyd Mk V. The diminutive carrier entered service in 1931 and it was used for transporting all manner of items and normally towed a small trailer. As with the Carden-Loyd, the engine and gearbox were located between the two-man crew, who had moveable rounded armoured covers over their heads. Stores were normally transported in the open rear compartment, while the tracked trailer could carry a 1,102lb load. A total of 6,700 were built by Renault, Fouga, AMX and Berliet. It was also used as a gun tractor, to tow a 25mm anti-tank gun, whilst a few were armed with machine guns and used by infantry combat units to provide mobile fire support. After the French surrendered, large numbers were taken over by the Wehrmacht and given the designation *Infanterie Schlepper UE 630(f)*. They were used for internal and airfield security work also as munition carriers (*Gepanzerter Munitionsschlepper UE (f)*). A few were armed with a 3.7cm PaK 35/36 anti-tank gun, while others in larger quantity, were issued to *Panzerpioneer* companies in 1943–44 and fitted with four *Wurfrahmen* 40

rockets for bombardment purposes. Finally, some were used as the basis for a wooden dummy tank. Specifications were: battle weight 2.64 tons, armour 4–7mm thick, engine: four-cylinder Renault 38hp petrol, top speed 30mph, range 112 miles. Dimensions: 9ft 3½ins long, 5ft 9½ins wide and 4ft 2ins high.

There was also a reasonable number of larger carriers built for the re-supply of tanks, for example, the Lorraine *Tracteur de ravitaillement*

Above: **The diminutive 2-ton Renault *Chenillette* was used for a wide variety of tasks. Much of its design was derived from the British Carden-Loyd.** *(TM)*

Right: **A total of 432, Lorraine *Tracteur de ravitaillement pour chars Modele 1937 L* (tank supply carriers) were built between 1939 and 1940. After the defeat of France, 350 were commandeered by the Germans.** *(GF)*

pour chars Modele 1937 L. The total order was for 432 and they were all built between January 1939 and May 1940. The Germans acquired over 350 of these after the defeat of France. Brief specifications of this 6.2 ton, two-man carrier were: length 14ft 1in, width 5ft 3¹/₂ins, and height 4ft 3¹/₂ins. Renault also produced a similar but smaller carrier a year earlier, the *Tracteur de ravitaillement pour chars Modele 1936 R.* This weighed only 2.5 tons and was 10ft 6ins long, 5ft 8¹/₂ins wide and 5ft 8¹/₂ins high. A total of 300 were built.

Right: **The most important Italian series of** *Semoventi* **(self-propelled artillery) included the 75/18 which mounted a 75mm howitzer. This 75/18 has been preserved at the Aberdeen Proving Ground (APG) Maryland, USA.** *(RJ Fleming)*

Right: **The** *Semovente* **75/18 da M40, was based on the chassis of the M13/40. The M41 was based on the M14/41 chassis and the M42 on the M15/42. This one was captured, during World War Two, in the Western Desert.** *(TM)*

171

Right: **The most widely deployed Italian armoured car was the AB 41, which mounted a 20mm gun and co-ax MG. It saw service on the Eastern Front as well as in North Africa, Italy and Hungary.**
(TM)

Left: **The smaller Semovente 47/32 su L6/40 mounted a 47mm anti-tank gun on the chassis of the L6/40 light tank.** *(RJ Fleming)*

Below: **About ninety of the larger *Semovente* M42/L da 105/25 SP guns were built, but sixty of them were commandeered by the Germans after the Italian surrender.** *(TM)*

Right: **The *Semovente* M43 DA 75/46 never saw Italian service, being built after the surrender in 1944/45 for the Germans (StuG M43 mit 75/46 852(i)). It mounted the powerful Italian 75/46 anti-aircraft gun.** *(TM)*

Left: **Also preserved at APG, the *Semovente* M 41M da 90/53, mounted a powerful 90mm gun on the rear of a turretless chassis. The four-man crew were dangerously exposed to enemy fire.** *(RJ Fleming)*

Below: **The *Semovente* da 149/40 would have been Italy's largest SP gun, but it never entered production. The 149mm gun was externally mounted and only six round of ammunition could be carried on the vehicle.** *(TM)*

CHAPTER SEVEN

Italy

Italy possessed some reasonable armoured cars and excellent tracked self-propelled guns which were used to good effect by both the Italians and later by the Germans.

During World War One, Italy had used well designed, reliable armoured cars (*Autoblindata* abbreviated to AB) and truck-mounted mobile anti-aircraft guns. They had also carried out some excellent experimental work on improving the performance of cross-country wheeled vehicles, between the wars, with the use of articulated chassis, all-wheel drive and very large wheels. However, World War Two found them very much in the same position as France, with a mixture of old, partly modernised World War One vehicles and a few more modern ones being introduced into service. Unlike France of course, they were able to perfect some good armoured cars during the early war years, whilst their self-propelled guns (*Semoventi*) were on the whole far better than their tanks and played an important direct fire rôle.

Scout & Armoured Cars

Italy did not produce a good scout car until late in World War Two, when around 250 *Lince* (Linx) were built by Lancia after the Armistice with Italy had been signed. In looks it was an almost exact copy of the British Daimler Dingo and was used by units of the *Republica Sociale Italiana* (*RSI*), the Fascist administration set up by Mussolini in Northern Italy during September 1943. It was armed with a single Breda 8mm

machine gun, weighed 3.14 tons and had a crew of two. Dimensions were 10ft 7ins long by 5ft 9½ins wide and 5ft 3½ins high.

The Bianchi AB 31 was an updated version of Bianchi's World War One armoured car modernised in 1931, the old Bianchi hull with an open-topped turret being mounted on a SPA 38 truck chassis fitted with pneumatic tyres. Designed for use in the Italian colonies in North Africa, it mounted a single machine gun and had very thin armour. They were easy prey for British armour in the Western Desert.

Dating back to World War One, some 4.3 ton six-man Lancia AB IZ armoured cars were still in service in Italian East Africa and possibly also in Libya, as it had been widely used in the Italian colonies between the wars.

Fiat Ansaldo began work on a new, large, six-wheeled, four-wheel drive armoured car in the early 1930s, based on the Fiat military truck. It had a crew of five and resembled the earlier Lancia AB IZ. The first model of the AB 611 produced in 1932, was only armed with four 8mm machine guns – twin forward firing and one rearward firing in the turret, plus another in the hull rear. The 611B, however, produced in 1934 mounted a 37mm gun in a seven-sided turret in place of the twin MGs. Weighing just under 7 tons, the five-man car was 15ft long, 6ft 2½ins wide and 7ft 9½ins high, with a top speed of 47 mph. It could also be driven at the same speed in

reverse. They were used operationally by Italian colonial forces in Ethiopia and East Africa.

The first prototype of Italy's new armoured car series AB 39/40, 41 & 43 was tested in mid-1939. It had four-wheel drive, with all four wheels independently sprung. It was fitted with dual-driving controls, one set at each end of the car, so that it could be driven in either direction – not a bad idea for a reconnaissance vehicle which had to get out of tight spots quickly, although it did waste valuable space through this duplication. The 6.85 ton, four-man AB 40 was armed with three 8mm Breda machine guns, two in the turret and one ball-mounted in the hull rear, firing over the back decks. It had spare wheels positioned on either side of the chassis, mounted on free bearings and located in such a position as to be able to assist in crossing difficult obstacles. Dimensions were 17ft 3½ins long, 6ft 5ins wide and 8ft 1in high.

Production of the AB 41 began in 1941, the main difference to its predecessor being that it mounted a 20mm gun with a co-ax machine gun in the turret instead of twin MGs. It was the most widely-used Italian armoured car of the war, seeing active service in North Africa, Italy, Hungary and the Soviet Union. Weight was now 7.4 tons and its top speed was just over 48mph. The final version, AB 43, mounted a 47mm gun weighed 7.47 tons, had a top speed of 56mph and a range of 334 miles. It was only built in limited quantity, production being ended by the

Italian surrender. It is estimated that approximately 550 of the AB-series were produced.

Armoured Personnel Carriers

Designed as a light armoured personnel carrier, the Carro Protetto AS 37 was based on the AS 37 four-wheel drive desert truck and could carry eleven men (including the driver) at about 30mph. It was armed with a single machine gun and weighed around 5 tons.

Self-propelled Guns

As well as various portée weapons, both AA and field, the Italians designed a number of wheeled SPs, such as the SPA 42, which had a 47mm gun, mounted on the open-topped chassis of the AB 41 armoured car, with a gunshield. Another was the *Autocanone Blindata Tipo 102*, which had a 102mm naval gun mounted on a low, six-wheeled armoured chassis, firing over the driver's cab. It had side armour, which could be lowered to allow the gun to traverse. Mention must also be made of the *Camionetta SPA 43*, which was a long, low 4 ton, four-wheeled vehicle mounting one or two 20mm AA guns, which could also be fired in the ground fighting rôle. It was designed for use in the desert by mechanised cavalry units on long

Above: **SPA Autoblindata (AB) 41's on patrol through a village in North Africa. Probably the best Italian armoured car of the war, it carried a crew of four and mounted a 20mm gun and co-ax MG.** *(TM)*

Right: **The *Lince* (Lynx) scout car was almost an exact copy of the Daimler Dingo and was built by Lancia. It was used by units of the Fascist *Republica Sociale Italiana*. (RSI).** (TM)

Below centre: **The Lancia IZM armoured car dates from 1917, however, it was deployed in Italian units during the Spanish Civil War. It was still in service in Italian East Africa and other parts of the Italian colonial empire at the start of World War Two.** (TM)

Below: **Rear view of the SPA AB 41. It was widely used in North Africa, the Soviet Union Italy and Hungary.** (TM)

range patrolling. It was also known as the *Sahariana Ante Aera SPA*.

I briefly mentioned the *Semoventi* in my companion book *World War Two Tanks*, because they really took the place of medium tanks in the Italian Army, however, for completeness they must also be mentioned here. The most important series, the *Semovente* 75/18, 75/32 or 75/34 da M 40, M 41 and M 42, was based upon the M13/40, M14/41 and M15/42 tank chassis, a box-like superstructure replacing the turret, while the main armament protruded through the front armour. All the series mounted a 75mm howitzer (either the 75/18, 75/32 or 75/34 model) as their main armament. In total 474 were built between 1941 to 1943 and they provided close artillery support for units

of Italian armoured divisions in North Africa, Sicily and Italy.

A number were commandeered by the Germans after the Italian surrender and these were designated by them *StuG M42 mit 75/18 850(i)* and *StuG M42 mit 75/34 851(i)* depending upon armament. Each vehicle could carry forty rounds of howitzer ammunition for the 75mm gun, which could traverse only twenty-five degrees to either side, so the vehicle had to track to engage targets outside of this arc. The vehicle carried a crew of three and was powered by a V8 SPA 15 TM 41 diesel or V8 15 TB petrol engine (dependent on type of chassis used), giving it a top speed of between 20 and 22mph with a range of approximately 125 miles. Dimensions depended upon type of

Right: **The *Camionetta SPA 43* were highly effective, long, low 4 ton vehicles, mounting a mixture of 20mm AA guns and machine guns. They were also ideal for long range patrol missions.** *(TM)*

chassis used, however, the largest the M42 was 16ft 9½ins long 7ft 5ins wide and 6ft 1in high, and weighed 15 tons.

In addition there was a command version, the *Carro Commando M41/M42* a turretless M14/41 or M15/42 tank with a heavy machine gun fitted on the righthand side of the driving position. A small number of around forty were known to have been built and some were taken over by the Germans after the surrender of Italy. Extra radio sets were fitted for command purposes. The vehicle weighed between 12.5 and 13.25 tons (depending on chassis used) and was normally crewed by four men.

Other *Semoventi* included:

Semovente 47/32 su L6/40 – Using the L6/40 light tank chassis, this 6.5 ton, 12ft 6ins long vehicle mounted a 47mm anti-tank gun on the left of a small, box-like superstructure with little space for the three-man crew or stowage although seventy rounds of ammunition were carried.

Nearly 300 were built between 1941 and 1942 for use in the Western Desert, but were quickly outclassed. Dimensions were: length 12ft 6ins, width 6ft 2½ins, height 5ft 7ins. It was powered by a four-cylinder SPA model 18 engine, had a top speed of 25mph and a range of 125 miles. After the surrender the Germans commandeered

Right: **The *Carro Commando Compagnia da 47/32*, was the company command version of the *Semovente L40 da 47/32*.** *(TM)*

Below: **Final model of the SPA Ansaldo series was the AB 43, which mounted a 47mm gun, and came into service in 1943.** *(TM)*

Left: **Ansaldo 90/55 gun model 41 on a Breda Tipo 51 heavy 6x4 truck chassis, fitted with six large side jacks for stability whilst firing. This one was abandoned in Sicily, August 1943.** *(TM)*

Left: **The *Semovente 75/18 da M40* was a straight conversion from the M13/40 tank, with a 75mm howitzer in a simple box-like superstructure.** *(TM)*

and dispatched some of those remaining to the Balkans to equip Croat forces.

Semovente M 41M da 90/53 – Less than thirty of these powerfully armed SPs were known to have been built. Designed specifically to deal with the Soviet T-34 medium tank but were never actually sent to the Eastern Front. The gun was mounted externally at the rear of the turretless chassis, which meant that the four-man crew were dangerously exposed to enemy fire. Stowage space was at a premium and only six rounds of ammunition could be carried on board for the Ansaldo M90/53 Model 39 dual-purpose gun, considered by some to be the best

Right: **The Semovente L40 da 47/32 mounted a 47mm anti-tank gun, which was obsolete by the time it entered service.** *(TM)*

Above: **The Semovente M42 da 75/18 was fitted with an SPA 15 TB M42 petrol engine and weighed approximately 20 tons.** *(TM)*

Italian anti-tank gun and comparable with the dreaded German 88mm. The vehicle weighed 17 tons and measured 17ft 1in long, 7ft 3ins wide and just under 7ft high. It was powered by a V8 SPA diesel and had a top speed of 21mph and a road range of 125 miles. The vehicles were used operationally in Sicily, the one remaining example is now at the Aberdeen Proving Ground, Maryland, USA.

Semovente M42L da 105/25 – A total of approximately ninety of these SP guns were built between 1943 and 1944, the initial thirty being delivered to the Italian Army, then after the surrender the Germans had an estimated further sixty built by Fiat-Ansaldo. Most of the original thirty were also acquired by the *Wehrmacht*. The 105mm gun was mounted in a box-like armoured superstructure on top of a specially widened M15/42 tank chassis, and was sometimes known as the M43. The 15.8 ton M42L had a crew of three, measured 16ft 9ins long, 8ft wide and 5ft 9ins high. It saw action in both Italy and the Balkans with

the Germans who designated it *Sturmgeschütz M43 mit 105/25 853(i)*.

Semovente da 149/40 which mounted a 149mm gun. Space was at such a premium that only six rounds of ammunition could be carried and only two of the crew (driver and commander) could ride in the vehicle, the rest having to travel in separate transport, together with extra ammunition. Only a prototype was ever built (now located at the Aberdeen Proving Ground), nevertheless, had Italy not surrendered it would have gone into production. It was a most effective SP and was designed to replace the towed 149/40 gun. It

weighed 24 tons, and measured 21ft 3½ins long, 10ft wide, 6ft 7ins high and was powered by a 250hp SPA petrol engine which gave it a top speed of 22mph.

The *Semoventi* were an effective part of the Italian artillery force, which had a good reputation and generally fought well. It is difficult to put an overall figure on numbers actually built, however, construction figures for the period 1940-43 totalled 526, so the wartime total can be estimated at around 800 to 850 for all types. Some of those taken over by the Germans were re-armed with a new weapon – the Italian 75/46 anti-aircraft gun and saw combat service.

CHAPTER EIGHT

Japan

More emphasis was placed on tanks in Japan than on armoured cars, although both armoured cars and halftrack vehicles were developed.

Encyclopedia of Armoured Cars by D Crow & R J Icks

Japan did not begin to start building cars and lorries seriously until the late 1920s, but even then the numbers produced were very small. However, with outside assistance from companies like Ford and General Motors, who established assembly plants in Japan, they did try to make up lost ground. By 1941, the annual output of civilian vehicles had risen to nearly 43,500 and presumably would have continued to rise had not the war intervened. The share of their wartime production capacity which the Japanese gave to the design and building of armoured fighting vehicles was never great, due to a deliberate policy to devote their main industrial capacity elsewhere. This was because they did not see armour as a battle winning weapon as the Germans did, but rather like the French, preferred to use it – if ever they did use it – for the close support of infantry. Armoured cars certainly had their uses, as they proved in the war against China, but the rôle of the armoured car for exploitation or for long distance reconnaissance, did not rate very highly in Japanese military thinking. Nevertheless, they did adapt their armoured cars for use on railway tracks, because in many countries in the Far East railways provided a far better and speedier means of traversing an area rather than using the often primitive roads and tracks. A major task for armoured cars in Manchuria, for example, was the protection of railway battalions from guerrillas and bandits.

To put the above quote into perspective one must also remember that the Japanese were never over concerned with the production of AFVs until well into the war, when they realised their mistake but, by that time it was too late to rectify matters. Nevertheless, they did produce some innovative vehicles for both the Imperial Navy and Army. Some of their armoured vehicles were deliberately designed from the outset so that they could be easily adapted to run on railway tracks as well as on roads. They also produced a small number of self-propelled guns, mounted on the *CHI-HA* medium tank chassis.

The Japanese also produced an interesting range of amphibians, work on them being largely carried out by the Imperial Japanese Navy. Details of these AFVs are to be found in the companion volume in this series: *World War Two Tanks* so they are not repeated here. In total, Japanese AFV production was insignificant compared with the other main protagonists of World War Two, especially as far as SP guns and other AFVs (less tanks) were concerned. One source puts the total of SPS and other AFVs at only 900 and even that is probably too optimistic. Mitsubishi, for example, built only fifty SP howitzers during the entire war. Many of the Japanese armoured cars had been purchased from abroad in the 1920s and 1930s (mainly from Britain, whilst cars used during World War Two were designed prewar.

Above: **An ex-British Indian pattern Vickers-Crossley, known as the Type 2587 (or Type 87), drives down a street in war-torn China watched by Japanese infantrymen.** *(TM)*

To understand the Japanese system of vehicle numbering one must first understand their calendar which began with the legendary founding of the Japanese Empire in 660 BC. To equate to our calendar one must always subtract 660. For example, the Type 2587 entered service in 1927 (subtract 660 from 2587 = 1927). Normally they used just the last two digits to signify the Type.

As far as vehicles markings are concerned, although many vehicles in the Japanese Army did carry markings, there was apparently no standardisation as is found in other armies, all insignia originating at divisional level or below, apparently at the whim of the commander, so these could change when commanders changed! Nevertheless, the national flag comprising the red disc (the Hi-No-Maru) on a white rectangle was used, but was only painted on Army vehicles. The Imperial Japanese Navy used the rising sun disc with red rays extending to the borders of the white rectangle. Examples of such flags will be seen in photographs in this chapter.

Armoured Cars

Japan's war against China had begun in 1937 and continued throughout World War Two, so some of their obsolescent armour was still in use during the war and was, for example, still listed in the official US Army *Handbook of Japanese Military Forces*. This was first published in 1942, then revised and expanded in 1944. The Type 2587 (or Type 87), which the Japanese purchased from Britain in 1927, is a case in point. Modernised by fitting pneumatic tyres, this version of the Indian pattern Vickers-Crossley was a reliable, if out-dated, six-wheeled AFV (two wheels at the front, four at the rear), weighing 5.4 tons, with a crew of four, armour 8mm thick mounting two Vickers .303in machine guns and powered by a four-cylinder 50 hp Crossley petrol engine which gave it a top speed of 40mph. It measured 16ft 6ins long, by 6ft 2½ins wide and 8ft 6ins high. The machine guns were ball-mounted, so they had limited individual traverse independent of the turret traverse.

Dating from 1928, the same year the Japanese car industry began, the Sumida Type ARM was built based on an Osaka lorry chassis with heavy spoked wheels and solid tyres. On top of the riveted, box-like hull was a conical-shaped turret housing a single machine gun. Osaka was also the location of the Japanese artillery arsenal. Like the Type 87 it was obsolescent by the start of World War Two.

There appear to have been both four-wheel and six-wheel Osaka Type 2592 armoured cars produced in 1932 and both were confusingly known as the Type 92. The four-wheeled Type 92 was a Japanese Army armoured car, the six-wheel version was built for the Japanese Navy. The four-wheel Type 92 did not look unlike

Right: **The Sumida Type 2593 (or Type 93) could be swiftly adapted for railway use, as seen here, supposedly in only ten minutes. Photographed on the Chinchow - Peipiao Railway, February 1938.**
(TM)

Below: **The Type 87 was modernised by fitting pneumatic tyres. This vehicle is in service with the Imperial Japanese Navy (note flag).**
(TM)

the Sumida ARM, but was armed with two machine guns, the one in the turret being mounted on a sliding traverse mount and fired through a long elongated slot. The vehicle weighed 6.4 tons with armour 8-11mm thick, had a crew of four and measured 16ft 5ins long, 6ft wide and 8ft 9ins high. Its four-cylinder 35hp engine gave it a top speed of 37mph and a range of 150 miles.

The latter Type 92, a 6x4, was more common. It weighed around 7tons, had a crew of up to six and mounted five machine guns – one in the turret, three in the hull (one in front and one each side) and one AA. Armour was 8-11mm thick, it was powered by a six-cylinder 85hp engine and allegedly had a top speed of 50mph. The vehicle was 15ft 9ins long, 6ft wide and 7ft 6ins high.

Used extensively in China, the Sumida Type 2593 (or Type 93) 6x4 was designed so that it could be easily adapted to either road or rail use.

Left: **The Sumida Type ARM dated from 1928, note the heavy spoked wheels and solid tyres.** *(TM)*

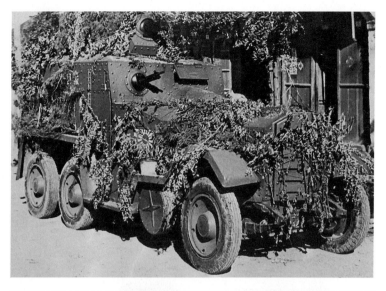

Top: **A well-camouflaged naval pattern Type 2592 (or Type 92), built in 1932 it weighed 6.2 tons and had a crew of six. Note the anti-grounding wheels behind the front wheels.** *(TM)*

Above: **A Sumida Type 2590, which like the Type 2593 was able to be adapted for railway use.** *(TM)*

On the rails it used six, flanged steel wheels. To be prepared for road use, it was jacked up on four built-in jack/roller units (mounted front and back), then solid rubber tyres (carried on the sides of the hull) were fitted and the vehicle driven off the railway track, using the short lengths of rail which were also carried on the hull, on to the road. It was claimed that this operation took only ten minutes to perform. The 7.5 ton, Type 93 had a crew of six, mounted a single machine gun in the turret, but there were weapon slits in the sides and a small observation hatch towards the rear of the roof of its large body. Dimensions were: 21ft 6ins long, 6ft 4ins wide and 9ft 9ins high. It had armour up to 16mm thick and top speeds of 25mph on roads and 37mph on rails.

Left: **The *HO-N II* mounted the long-barrelled 75mm Type 90 gun in an open-topped turret.** *(TM)*

Above: **Built in 1943, the *HA-TO* mounted an enormous 300 mm trench mortar on the open rear deck.** *(TM)*

Far right: **A group of Japanese infantrymen ride on a Sumida Type 2593 armoured car, adapted for railway use.** *(TM)*

Below: **The *SO-KI* twin 20mm anti-aircraft guns on a lengthened *KYU-GO* chassis.** *(TM)*

Armoured Personnel Carriers

A small number of long-bodied armoured personnel carriers were built during the 1930s, using both Ford and Bedford chassis. All had armour-plated radiator covers with ventilation louvres, a long box-like armoured hull, rear door(s), and in some cases escape hatches in the roof and an anti-grenade fence around the top.

Self-propelled Guns

Japan produced a number of satisfactory SP guns – one figure given for Mitsubishi Industries' wartime production being fifty – mainly based upon the Type 97 *CHI-HA* medium tank chassis. Most common were the *HO-NI I, II and III*. The first of these mounted a 75mm anti-tank gun in a fixed, open-topped turret and was developed in 1942. It weighed about 14.6 tons, had a crew of three and was powered (as the tank) with a 170hp Mitsubishi V12 diesel

engine, which gave it a top speed of 25mph and a range of 131 miles. Approximate dimensions were 18ft 3ins long, by 7ft 9ins wide and 7ft 9½ins high. The gun had some twenty degrees of traverse and could elevate from minus five degrees to plus twenty degrees. The five-man, 1.5 ton heavier *HO-NI II*, was armed with short-barrelled 105mm howitzer, while the *HO-NI III* was identical except that it was fitted with a 75mm Type 88 anti-tank gun and had slightly better armoured protection at the top and rear of the gunshield.

A larger calibre SP was the Type 38 *HO-RO*, which also used the *CHI-HA* chassis, but mounted the larger 150mm howitzer which had a range of nearly 6000 metres, could elevate thirty degrees, but had only eight degrees of traverse. It weighed approximately 15 tons, had a square box-like turret and measured 18ft long, 7ft 8½ins wide and 7ft 9ins high.

Other SPs, reportedly built for the Japanese Navy, included types mounting either a 120mm and 200mm naval gun, both again using the *CHI-HA* chassis.

Anti-aircraft Tanks

The Japanese made some attempts to produce anti-aircraft mounts to fit on both their light and medium tank chassis in open-topped superstructures, but none were used in action. However, there was the *SO-KI*, which mounted either a single or twin 20mm AA cannons on the light tank chassis. Also the *SA-TO*, which mounted a 20mm cannon on an open-topped *CHI-HA* medium tank chassis. Finally, there was the *TA-HA* which mounted twin 37mm AA guns on a medium tank chassis, but it is believed that this project was never completed.

Armoured Trains

Like the Soviet Union, the Japanese used armoured trains, although theirs were by no means as elaborate as the Soviet models. The basis was principally armoured freight cars, the general model mounting four machine guns and with space to carry up to twenty fully-equipped riflemen. There were also other freight cars adapted to carry artillery guns (up to 75mm), machine gun cars, command cars and even trucks carrying the equipment to repair damaged sections of track. The train was drawn by an armoured locomotive and would be made up from a mixture of the various types of armoured freight trucks as the situation required.

CHAPTER NINE

Other Countries

It is to overcome the obvious handicap under which unarmoured cars labour that, time and again, armour protection has been improvised for them.

Armour by Richard M Ogorkiewicz

f course other countries of the world designed and built their own AFVs in addition to sometimes using those produced by the main combatants. This was possible because armoured cars were much easier to design and manufacture than tanks, whilst self-propelled guns could be adapted from existing AFVs. Without doubt the best were those designed and built by Sweden, whilst the strangest were the improvised armoured cars built by the underground resistance forces of neighbouring Denmark, which in many ways resembled the similarly locally manufactured British Home Guard armoured cars (see Chapter 1) or the older and even odder-looking *Camion Blindado* of the Spanish Civil War. Not all these AFVs saw action, while others were merely used for Internal Security work in occupied countries, however, they do provide a glimpse of the other interesting AFVs which were in existence during World War Two.

AUSTRIA

Some of the earliest armoured cars in the world, for example, the Daimler *Panzerwagens* of 1904 and 1905 which were the first turreted armoured cars, had been designed and built in Austria who had possessed the technical ability from before World War One and went on building many more successful vehicles during that

war. However, the Versailles Treaty forbade them to build any more AFVs except for a small number of wheeled armoured cars for their own police force. Despite the ban, by the early 1930s the Austro-Daimler Company had begun to design and build new armoured cars in secret, producing their massive 11.5 ton 8x8 ADGZ in 1933.

When Austria like Germany renounced the Treaty it was followed in to production by the ADGZ 1935, which was a much improved version of the model they had built in secret. It carried both light and heavy machine guns in a larger, rounder turret, plus two more heavy machine guns in ball mountings at the front and rear of the hull. The well-shaped vehicle was of welded construction and had drive to all eight wheels. It weighed 8 tons and was 20ft 6ins long, 6ft 11ins wide and 8ft 5½ins high. They then went on to produce a second type of armoured car, the 6x6 ADKZ in 1938, which had flat, well-rounded mudguards running along the entire length of the vehicle, a radio antenna around the turret and ball mountings for both turret and hull-mounted machine guns. It measured 15ft 6ins long, 7ft 11ins wide and 8ft high. At the front was a large roller which was intended to help the vehicle to transit obstacles when travelling cross-country. The Germans no doubt made use of these vehicles when they annexed Austria, but possibly only for internal security and police duties.

Above: **Austrian ADGZ 1935 armoured cars on parade in Vienna. Weighing some 8 tons they mounted both heavy and light machine guns and were fitted with the Voith-Getriebe torque converter transmission.** *(TM)*

Three lighter vehicles are worthy of mention: the ADSK *Kleinerpanzerwagen*, a small 4x4 scout car without a turret, built in 1937; the even smaller ADSK Baby also built in 1937 and the diminutive ADMK *Mulus* wheel-cum-track machine gun carrier, built in 1935.

BELGIUM

Despite playing a major part in the development of armoured cars in World War One, the Belgian Army had only a handful of relatively modern armoured cars in service at the start of World War Two, having purchased twelve French built Berliet VUDBs in 1930. They were used by both the two light regiments of the Gendarmerie and retired from service in May 1940. One Berliet VUDB 4 was also delivered to the Belgian Army in 1930-31 as a prototype but none were purchased.

In early 1940, the Belgians also used a form of partly armoured civilian van (the Ford/Marmon Herrington armoured van) which was built on an American Ford 1-ton chassis. The armoured shell was manufactured in Belgium and the vehicle assembled at the Ford works at Antwerp. It was intended as a towing vehicle for the 47mm anti-tank gun in cavalry regiments. The Germans took over those which remained after Belgium surrendered. The Free Belgium Forces in Britain were re-equipped

with a mixture of British and American vehicles, the first being the Guy Mk 1A armoured car which was supplied to their armoured squadron, when the unit was formed in 1940.

Built under licence in Belgian were a number of British Carden-Loyd light 2-ton tractors, which the Belgium Army used for towing the 47mm anti-tank gun in both cavalry and infantry units. There were two types, with or without seats for personnel. The Germans also took over the remaining Utility B tractors, giving them the designation *Artillerieschlepper VA 601(b)*.

The T13 (Type1) self-propelled gun was designed utilising the chassis of the Vickers Carden-Loyd Type1 tractor. It mounted a 47mm gun, in a fixed half-turret with shutters, which fired over the rear decks. The vehicle had a crew of three, weighed 4.5 tons and had armour 9mm thick. Dimensions were 12ft 2$^{1}/_{2}$ins long, 6ft wide and 4ft 6ins high and had a top speed of 25mph.

The T13 (TypeIII), used the Carden-Loyd TypeIII tractor chassis, but differed from the Type1 in both suspension and transmission. The 47mm gun was mounted in a half turret with all-round traverse. The vehicle weighed 5 tons and was very similar in size to the TypeI. A total of 150 of both types of T13 were built in Belgium, the TypeIII being deployed mainly in cavalry and infantry units also with border cyclist patrol troops.

Right: **In 1933, the Austro-Daimler Company secretly began to design the ADGZ, an 8x8 armoured car, which was completed in 1934,** *(TM)*

Right: **The 6x6 ADGZ armoured car was produced in 1938 and had a very large turret ventilator placed between the two machine gun ball mountings. Note the frame aerial and the front rollers.** *(TM)*

DENMARK

Like other near neighbours of Sweden, before World War Two, Denmark purchased a small number of the excellent Swedish-built armoured cars. These were the L185 armoured car of 1933 built to Danish specifications and the more modern 1939 Lynx armoured car. Fortunately the numbers were small and Sweden only delivered three of the eighteen Lynx ordered. Those that remained in working order, once the country was occupied, were used by the German police.

Above: The ADSK
Baby scout car
look very like
the 1937
*Kleinerpanzer-
wagen*, except for
the stepped front.
(TM)

Left: The
diminutive ADMK
Mulus wheel-cum-
track, machine
gun carrier could
run on tracks or
on roadwheels
(stored at the rear
of vehicle). (TM)

The Danish Resistance did build an improvised armoured car in 1945 using a Ford truck
chassis. They called it the Holger-Danske V-3
– a joke against the Germans because of their
V-1 and V-2 rockets. The armoured car was
used to support attacks by the Holger-Danske
section of the Resistance.

EIRE

Eire (Republic of Ireland) was a neutral country in World War Two and had purchased a
number of modern armoured cars from
Sweden in the early 1930s, to replace their

Above: **The Holger-Dansk V-3 was produced in 1945 by a Danish Resistance unit of the same name.** *(TM)*

Above centre: **Berliet VUDB armoured cars, in service with the Belgian Army, are paraded through Brussels in 1939.** *(TM)*

Right: **Built in 1938, on the Carden-Loyd T-13 light tank chassis, this Belgian close support SP mounted a 47mm gun offset to the left in a half turret.** *(TM)*

ageing World War One type Rolls-Royce, Peerless and Lancia vehicles. Eight L180s were purchased and a further fourteen ordered, however, the outbreak of war prevented delivery. In addition the Irish built four armoured cars based on a Leyland Terrier chassis and fitted with Swedish-built Landswerk L60 tank turrets. These entered service with the 1st Armoured Car Squadron in 1939 and were still in use up to the 1980s. One is on display in the Tank Museum at Bovington.

During 1940/41 28 Ford MkVI were built to a design by Colonel Lawless and Commandant Mayne of the Cavalry Corps. Post-war some were used in the congo in 1961.

HUNGARY

Nicholas Straussler, who is best remembered for his invention of the Duplex Drive for amphibious tanks, designed a number of arm-oured cars

for Britain between the wars. He also designed the Csaba 39 Mpcgk for his home country of Hungary. It was a good looking three-man armoured car, built in 1939 mounting a 20mm gun and co-ax machine gun in a well shaped, centrally placed turret. Dimensions were 14ft 9ins long, 6ft 10½ ins wide and 7ft 5ins high. It is thought that they were used by the Germans for internal security duties in Hungary.

The Hungarians also produced a very successful self-propelled assault gun version of their *Turan* medium tank, the *Zrinyi II*, which mounted a 10.5cm howitzer. It was designated as the *40/43 M Zrinyi Rolamloveg* in Hungarian Army service. Over sixty were built, the main armament being a 10.5cm 40/43 M L/20.5 (MAVAG) howitzer for which fifty-two rounds of ammunition were carried. The 21.5 ton vehicle carried a crew of four and measured 19ft 8ins long, 9ft 8ins wide and 7ft 3½ins high, armour was 13-75mm thick. Top speed was 27mph with a range of 137 miles. The Hungarian

Right: **The Csaba 39 Mpcgk was the only Hungarian armoured car to be designed by Nicholas Straussler. It had a faceted turret mounting a 20 mm gun and co-ax MG.** *(TM)*

Far right top: **The Dutch M38 was in fact the Swedish Landswerk L182, purchased from Sweden in the 1930s.** *(TM)*

Far right centre: **The Polish-built Ursus Wz 29 was a conventional looking armoured car which bristled with armament – a 37 mm gun and three machine guns.** *(TM)*

Right: **The Dutch M39 *Panserwagen*, was the production model of the Van Dorne Type 3 armoured car.** *(TM)*

Far right: **Another version of the Polish-built Ursus, the Wz 34, also mounted a 37mm gun.** *(TM)*

Army were also issued with 100 *Hetzers* by the Germans.

Netherlands

Although in 1939 Dutch armoured car strength was only thirty-six in total, they were all quite modern and fully operational armoured vehicles equal to anything that the Germans had in service. They had twelve each of the M-36 and M-38 armoured cars, which were in fact Swedish Landswerk 180 and 182.

However, they also had twelve DAF M39 *Panserwagen 38*, a modern-looking 6x4, 6-ton armoured car mounting a 20mm cannon and co-ax machine gun in the turret and two more machine guns in the front and rear of the hull. In 1937 it first appeared in prototype form as the Van Dorne Type 3. Noticeable features were large engine cooling louvres on the top of the hull at the rear and small roller wheels at the front to prevent the low-slung hull from bellying when crossing obstacles. The M39 was 15ft 5ins long, 6ft 8½ ins wide and 6ft 8½ ins high. The Germans commandeered them when Holland was occupied and used them for internal security duties, designating them *Panderspähwagen DAF 201(h)*.

Some improvised armoured cars, APCs and AA lorries were also used in the Dutch East Indies, but only in small numbers.

POLAND

Poland had to face the might of the German *Blitzkrieg* with a handful of outdated tanks and armoured cars. The latter were the elderly Ursus Wz 29 built in 1926 and the slightly more modern Ursus Wz 34 I & II. The Wz 29 mounted a 37mm Puteaux gun in the turret, plus a machine gun in a separate mounting, pointing out of the left-hand side of the turret. A second machine gun was located at the rear of the hull. Disc wheels with pneumatic tyres were fitted. Dimensions were 17ft long, by 6ft wide and 8ft 1in high. The Wz 34 had a shorter, stubbier hull (under 12ft long), while the turret had a cupola on top. Main turret armament was either the 37mm gun or a heavy machine gun.

ROMANIA

Prior to the war the Romanian Army purchased some Czechoslovak-built tanks including 126 of their LT vz 35 light tanks (designated by Romania as the R-2 light tank) these were

Right: **The excellent 1939 Swedish-built Lynx scout car, which weighed 8 tons and had a top speed of almost 45mph.** *(TM)*

deployed successfully in Russia with the 1st Royal Armoured Division, but suffered heavy casualties at Stalingrad in March 1943. After withdrawing them from front line service some were converted to self-propelled guns by fitting captured Soviet 7.62cm M42 guns in an open-topped structure.

SWEDEN

Although the Swedes maintained strict neutrality during the war, some of their armoured cars saw action with other combatants, for example the Dutch had both the Landswerk 180 and 182 in service, the Danes both the Landswerk 185 and Lynx.

The Landswerk 185 was a 4x4 armoured car, built in 1933 and based on a Ford car chassis with disc wheels and a long bonnet with distinctive engine cooling louvres. Mounting a 20mm gun and two machine guns, the 4.2-ton vehicle had a top speed of 37mph and a range of just over 90 miles. Its dimensions were 16ft long, 5ft 9ins wide and 9ft 1in high.

In 1938 the very streamlined 4x4 Lynx, which weighed 8 tons, first appeared. The production model of 1939 was not quite so streamlined but was a highly effective vehicle, remaining in Swedish service until long after the end of World War Two. It had a larger turret than the original model, with a hinged cupola, but still mounted the 20mm gun and three machine guns (one co-ax and two in the hull - one at the front and one in the rear). The 16ft 9ins long vehicle was 7ft 6ins wide and 7ft 2½ ins high, had a top speed of 44mph and a range of 155miles.

The Landswerk 180, 181 and 182 armoured cars were based on the 6x4 Scania-Vabis truck chassis, with a front-mounted engine and a well-shaped, conventional looking turret. Armament was a 20mm Madsen cannon and a co-ax machine gun, plus another MG alongside the driver. Top speed was 50mph and the range 180 miles. All had a crew of four or five men, weighed between 6 and 7 tons and measured just over 18ft long, by 6ft 6ins wide and 8ft high.

The L30 wheel-cum-track, also built by Landswerk, never entered full production but was an interesting vehicle which, it was claimed, could switch from wheels to tracks in under thirty seconds whilst the vehicle was actually moving! It had the M 31 light tank turret and was sometimes known as the Strv fm/31. It weighed 11.5 tons, had a top speed on wheels of 47mph and a range of 187 miles. Main armament was a 37mm gun.

Top: **The Swedish-built Landswerk 181 armoured car used a Scania Vabis 6x4 truck chassis and mounted a 20mm gun in conventional looking turret.** *(TM)*

Above: **The Landswerk 182 was the third model of the series which started in production as the 180. All weighed between 6 and 7 tons.** *(TM)*

Left: **The Landswerk 185 light armoured car was based on a Ford passenger car chassis. It weighed 4.2 tons and mounted a 20 mm gun and two machine guns.** *(TM)*

Sweden built a number of very useful looking self-propelled guns (*Stormartillerivagen (Sav)*) based on the Strv m/41 tank chassis which was of course the Czech TNH-Sv built under licence. One of these was the Sav m/43, the prototype of which mounted a 75mm Bofors gun. The production model built by Scania-Vabis was armed with a new 105mm Sak m/44 gun but only eighteen were produced. Other Savs built on the m/41 chassis were the PvKv 3 mounting a 57mm anti-tank gun, the PvKv 4 which mounted the 75mm L/60 AA gun, both in open-topped turrets, whilst an earlier PvKv 2 was based on the Swedish designed Strv m/40 with a 57mm gun mounted in an armoured sleeve.

Index

Reference to photographs shown in *italics*

A US Army convoy, led by two M8 HMC self-propelled howitzers, passes down a country lane in England, May 1945. (TM)